DOWN TO EARTH
with
HELEN DILLON

DOWN TO EARTH
with
HELEN DILLON

TIMBER PRESS

Published in North America in 2007 by
Timber Press, Inc.
The Haseltine Building
133 S.W. Second Avenue, Suite 450
Portland, Oregon 97204-3527 U.S.A.
www.timberpress.com

A catalog record for this book is available from
the Library of Congress.

ISBN-13: 978-0-88192-859-4

Printed and bound in China

9 8 7 6 5 4 3 2 1

Contents

Introduction

SHOULDN'T HAVE

We've all done something we shouldn't have. I shouldn't have eaten that whopping bit of cheese. I shouldn't have worn that dress, as I look like a sofa in it. At least a sofa is useful, unlike my cast-cement birdbath with robin perched delicately on the edge, which I shouldn't have bought in the first place. Somebody stole the robin, which was essential to the balance, so the bath keeps falling over, there's no water in it and the birds are confused. Would the person who took the robin please bring it back and take the birdbath instead?

Mind you, the birdbath is by no means the ultimate in tacky. I think the worst, largest and most expensive object we ever had, in the mid-1970s, was a 2.7m/9ft tall, 2.7m/9ft wide cast-iron four-tiered Victorian fountain decorated with herons and flowers, the whole thing covered in many different layers of gloss paint, mostly white, flaking off in patches to reveal a striking, swimming-pool turquoise. Water was pumped to the top and from there it frothed and sparkled down to the next layer, dripping from the wings of herons and tumbling over the scalloped rims of each basin, until it reached the 2.7m/9ft diameter cast-iron saucer, also frilled at the edges, in which a single goldfish swam gloomily round and round, through various oxygenating plants, none of which seemed to clear the water. I didn't like to get him any companions, as he was already lopsided, because of a sinister-looking bulge, and looked as if he might capsize at any moment. I was also concerned that new fish would catch his bulge, whatever it was. Eventually, to everyone's relief, a visiting heron (real) ate him.

I learnt an important lesson over that fountain in that I tried every possible means of disguise, to reduce the dominance it had over the garden, and nothing, but nothing, did the trick. In all its gleaming magnificence, its height, its glaring whiteness, its fancy cake-decoration flounces and frills, there it was, a shining beacon of bad taste right in the middle of the garden. I planted evergreen bushes to right and left; I encircled it in a low box hedge; I draped it in

Too chocolate-boxy for words: rose 'Madame Grégoire Staechelin' was dug up suffering from blackspot, *Lonicera periclymenum* 'Graham Thomas' swamped everything and now grows as a standard elsewhere. All four box balls have gone — they looked very 1980s and smug. The statue is now turned sideways and looks as if she's fleeing from the scene.

The garden in my municipal park period, *circa* 1979 – you can just see the wedding cake fountain in the distance.

variegated ivies; I tried flowerbeds round it, gravel round it, lawn round it. Neither Val, my husband, nor I liked to admit to the other that we didn't like it. Eventually – another great source of relief – a London garden furniture dealer came and took it away.

My friend Feargus McGarvey has a wonderful remark for describing the phenomenon of trying to disguise something that doesn't – and never will – work: 'However much lipstick you put on it, it's still a gorilla.' (He says his colleague, Gerry Mitchell, should always be given credit for this most useful of sayings.)

The figure at the end of the garden, which I understand is of Diana, is made of some kind of late nineteenth-century stone substitute. She's nothing special, as well as being short of an arm, but makes a satisfactory focal point. I sometimes think that stone and marble figures, whatever their date and value, from Renaissance to reproduction cement, are really just toys for grown-ups. I'm now thinking of swapping her with the marble urn, which is soothingly plain and eighteenth century, positioned at the moment under the overhanging branches of next door's yew. Diana did cause a bit of a stir when we first had a write-up in a British Sunday paper, and we naively thought that from then on we'd have masses of visitors. But the net result was a call from Brighton CID to say that a local lady in her nineties was claiming that the statue belonged to her. (We had bought it at James Adam's auction rooms, Stephen's Green, Dublin, twenty years prior to that.) The pair of sphinxes are made of Coadestone, a rare stone substitute invented by a woman, Mrs Coade, in the eighteenth century, for which the recipe has been lost. These are rather good, except every time there's frost, which isn't often here in Dublin, another hunk flakes off.

Now comes the pompous bit. I went to a garden recently where the owner had obviously come under the influence of a dubious antique dealer. I have never seen so many objects in a garden. They were made of terracotta, of glazed Oriental pottery, of iron, of lead, of suspect metals made to look like lead, of bronze and stuff that was meant to look like it and wood of every sort. There were things that hung on walls, containers that were originally made for holding hay in stables and reproductions of same, and wall plaques with languid Art Nouveau young women surrounded by wreaths of grapes and vine leaves. Of objects to do with water there were many – Grecian urns on their sides from which water flowed, giant pottery teapots; and there were mysterious spouts of water gushing from positions on walls from whence there was no reason whatsoever that water should gush.

Whoever was influencing the owner of this garden – or perhaps the owner himself – had an overruling passion for cherubs. There were rounded fat bottoms and sweet little feet and wings simply everywhere – I didn't know where to look for cherubims and seraphims, a plethora of putti and a general gathering of cherubic beings. And there were quantities of ladies, none wearing much, from shepherdesses and irritating little girls dressed as fairies to Grecian ladies looking like the cast of *Up Pompeii*, including the late, great Frankie Howerd. And I haven't even started on the Bambis, squirrels, frogs with disturbing smiles, giant tortoises and toadstools in various sizes. There were summerhouses, and more summerhouses that moved round in circles, Wendy houses, garden sheds, arches, arch-covered seats, swings and gazebos galore.

How I would love to throw all the toys out of the pram! All of them. In one great sweep. My theory, pompous or otherwise, is that more is definitely less, and you shouldn't be able to see more than one item, which includes any of the above-mentioned ornaments, including my own, in one sweep of the eye. Except, perhaps, a grouping of pots that looks like one feature, or a series of the same pots, statues, etc., arranged formally. That is not to say, much as I loved the film, that I want to see a formal series of Bambis.

Apart from the famous gorilla remark above, I think the most useful thing I was ever told was about the view of a border. This is obvious if you've heard it before, but not if you've never thought about it: if you're looking at a border, or a piece of planting face on – for example, if you're looking out of the main windows of your house at a border that's parallel to the house, directly opposite the window – it is difficult to get the view of the planting right; whereas if you are looking at borders at right angles to the house, if there's a great gap in the planting, you'll barely notice. You can fiddle around with the parellel border and despair of ever getting it right, whereas the borders at 90 degrees can have some unfortunate plantings and it won't matter one bit.

Next time you go out to the garden, just say to yourself, looking at every single object, from pot to arch to seat and back, 'Perhaps I shouldn't have . . .' There's often the problem, in an inherited garden, that you don't think of moving something because it's always been there. Last week I was in a beautiful garden overlooking Dublin Bay, with a mostly original 1820s garden. Plumb in the middle of the view was a garden seat, raised on a plinth, on which to sit and look out to sea. A charming idea, and lovely to see the view if you're sitting on the seat, but from the distance of the house it looked like a small boil on the bottom of a large landscape. I'm delighted to hear it's being moved.

THE EVOLUTION OF A GARDEN

When Val and I arrived here at 45 Sandford Road, Ranelagh, Dublin, thirty-six years ago I didn't want to change a thing. Everything seemed enchanting – the rockery, the rose beds, the iris bed, the lot, especially the sunny aspect and the comparatively large size for a city garden (a bit more than half an acre).

But we'd hardly moved in before we decided that the rockery would have to go. However well it mimicked Nature, what was a sudden rocky outcrop doing in the middle of a completely flat Dublin garden? Off it went, in a series of skips. We were then lacking a focal point, so the builders who were doing up the house built a circular pool (about 2m/7ft in diameter) at the end of the lawn on an axis from the house. It was barely filled up with water for the first time when we came across the Victorian cast-iron fountain I described earlier, in a Glasgow antique shop. We couldn't wait to buy it. We rushed home and filled up the pond with rubble. After a long trip in a furniture van, and much heaving and puffing, we finally plonked the fountain down on top. So good was it as a focal point that, as I said, everything else melted into the background. It was an expensive mistake.

Weeding in the iris bed was a balancing act involving standing on one leg and getting bad-tempered and pulling the tops off weeds that refused to budge. Right, I thought, man (or certainly woman) is a higher being than a weed; I'll get the better of them. So Sean (a taxi driver turned gardener) and I turned the iris bed into lawn and paved a small area up on the right, leaving 0.5m/2ft square beds for the irises. To begin with, smug as could be, the newly divided irises remained free of weeds. Then the weeds quietly got on with what weeds are good at doing: infiltrating the space of other plants. End of that idea. This area became a terraced area with box hedging, angel's fishing rods (dieramas) and a lead cherub.

We then realized that the main terrace near the house was so narrow that we all sat there in a row, as if in a doctor's waiting room. All we could see were the prickly stems of the roses in the bed directly in front of the terrace. You couldn't see the garden from there, and you couldn't access it unless you walked to the end of the terrace and up a narrow path. So the unthinkable happened: we had the courage to remove the phalanx of roses and double the width of the terrace. After weeks of telephoning salvage firms, Val managed to acquire some old granite steps to put in the middle of the terrace, leading up to the lawn.

Meanwhile, apart from endlessly digging up convolvulus (weedkiller wasn't an option, as Sean couldn't understand the labels on bottles), I was having an amazingly happy time, recklessly buying plants, planting them in the nearest gaps and rushing out to buy more. I had new gardening friends, who gave me plants and 'slips' (which in Ireland can mean anything from a cutting to a big piece of plant, roots and all). Available space in the beds was filling up. The queue of plants waiting to be positioned grew longer. We needed more space.

Heleniums, fennel and *Canna* 'Musifolia' in the red border

So, around 1979, we took up both sides of the lawn to make the two main borders that still exist today. At the same time, we laid out an oval lawn at the far end on the left (the soil was overused and no good for veg) and gradually completed a semicircle of arches and tunnel to the end of the garden. But it wasn't until around 1985 that a visit from a well-known London garden furniture dealer gave us both, simultaneously, the idea of selling the Victorian fountain. We reinstated the pool by removing the rubble and filling it up with water. It is still here, at the end of the canal, except now, following a visit to Morocco, where we saw wonderful shallow pools, it is only 7cm/3in deep.

Circa 1975 we built a raised circular bed surrounding a nineteenth-century Irish sundial at the far end of the garden, separated by a metal trellis from the small paved area for irises. This bed is for small, special plants that cannot tolerate being crowded and need full sun and good drainage, useful for my New Zealand daisies (celmisias), a well-established *Tropaeolum polyphyllum* (prostrate), the scarce South American nasturtium and small early bulbs. In autumn 2003 we transformed the oval lawn at the end into a gravel garden, planted with many members of the *Araliaceae* family and plants with big leaves. There's a seat tucked away up there, a place to go and sit and think.

The alpine house (a small lean-to greenhouse with masses of ventilation all year) was built in 1990 for alpines, auriculas, South African bulbs and suchlike that dislike winter wet. This area is important as an interim space for hardening off plants on their way from greenhouse to garden.

The front garden was a gloomy laurel thicket sloping down from the front door to the gate when we arrived. So we took everything out, dug the soil and laid a path through it in a sweeping curve. But I was never happy with it, as I felt that to suit the formality of a late Regency (1830) house, we needed a level rather than a sloping surface. Thus in 1996 we had a huge upheaval, in which we levelled the front, supported it with a retaining wall and paved it in Donegal sandstone. Feargus McGarvey, my landscape architect friend, suggested that we should put down a large square of paving in front of the house. Much as I hated losing so much planting space, I like this simple, empty piece of paving with nothing on it. Just looking at it clears my head of clutter.

In 2005 we re-did the front again and repaved the large square in Chinese granite, as in order to save money the first time we had used pieces of sandstone that were too small and had shifted; larger pieces of stone not only look better but are also more secure. Up until then the planting had been very 1960s looking, a hotchpotch of one of this and one of that; so we took it all up and, influenced by a visit to the Blue Steps, at the iconic modernist Fletcher Steele garden at Naumkeag, Massachusetts (a series of blue pools descending a gentle slope, flanked by flights of steps, set in a grove of birches and underplanted with ferns), we planted fifty-one birch trees. These are mostly the cultivar *Betula* 'Fascination' (20m/65ft), bred by Jan Ravensburg here in Ireland.

The biggest upheaval of all took place in 2000, when we took up the lawn and replaced it with a canal set in Irish limestone. The seed of the idea was sown in the 1980s, when Rosemary Verey (while in Ireland to give a talk) remarked that a rill down the centre of the lawn might look good. Visits to Morocco, India and especially the Court of the Myrtles at the Alhambra in Spain must have further embedded the notion. The classic simplicity of buildings and reflections very much appeals to me. Apart from relieving us of the need to mow the lawn (and water, feed, edge and aerate the grass), the plain expanse of water and limestone, which remains completely static, means that the planting in the borders at the sides can be more informal, as if the plants are relaxing in the sun.

This is the much abbreviated story of the structure of the garden at 45 Sandford Road. But the story of the plants, and all those that I've loved and lost, is a long and romantic parallel tale that runs alongside. They are the survivors of several purges, or they have been edited out years ago and then reinstated as I've come late to appreciate their charms. The plants that still grow here are special.

The canal at tulip time. The pots in the foreground are planted with cornflowers, waiting to take the place of the tulips.

Part I

BEGINNERS' STUFF

Structure

I've always had problems with the word 'structure', implying as it does strict rules and the laying down of the law. But, I suppose, without structure in the garden all you'd have would be a charming wilderness, in which you'd wander around meeting dead ends, tripping over plants and colliding with bushes, and where – like Alice – you might disappear down a rabbit hole.

The first structure you have to consider is what surrounds your garden. Is it a wall, a hedge, a fence or nothing at all? Do you like it? Is it high enough? Could you afford to change it? If it's a wall, is it tall enough? (Check your area regulations for maximum height allowed.) Perhaps you could increase its height by putting a wooden trellis above it. If so, the trellis idea needs more thought – do you want to use cheap trellis (which usually looks untidily finished) or order some expensive, good-quality hardwood that fades to beautiful silvery grey? And if you'd like a hedge, do you live in a city and need the formality of a yew, beech or hornbeam hedge, or do you want the country look of a hawthorn, holly or mixed hedge? Or perhaps you don't need an actual division between you and next-door neighbours, but an informal group of small trees such as birch or (in mild areas) a grove of myrtles, to act as a screen and windbreak.

Neighbours are a delicate subject. You'd be amazed how often on a garden advice visit I find that the garden owner gets on perfectly with the neighbours on one side but has a problem with the residents on the other side. Europeans seem to have an inherent desire to fence their property in (and are prepared for savage arguments in court about every boundary inch), whereas in other countries (the USA in particular) gardens are open plan. Personally, I care so much about how much sun and light the garden gets that nothing else matters. In other words, I'd rather see the neighbours than be shaded by trees.

Clematis 'Perle d'Azur' drapes itself over iron arches made in the 1970s. We originally made the circular pool 90cm/3ft deep, but then I noticed – in Morocco – how effective shallow water is, so we reduced the depth to 7cm/3in – much to the delight of local blackbirds.

Your next structural decision, after you have thought about the surrounds of the garden, is whether to divide up the garden itself, not necessarily into the obvious, ever-mentioned 'rooms' but perhaps into a series of informal spaces leading through the garden. In the best gardens, your feet seem to unconsciously find their way around, and, with neither arrow nor signpost, you find yourself back at the beginning. In a small garden you may need no more than some tall grasses or shrubs, echoed on the other side, to delineate, for instance, a paved, outdoor living area from a more relaxed play or vegetable area towards the back of the garden.

Probably the biggest decision on structure is about your terrace or patio – or whatever you call the area you sit on at the sunny side of your house. (I suppose you could say if it's outside the lounge you call it the patio and if it's outside the drawing room you call it the terrace. You might, indeed, call it a living room.) How big this should be and of what it should be made you should seriously think about. When we installed our first terrace it was far too narrow, had an annoying slope and was made of concrete – in those days, the early 1970s, it wasn't done to show off by using real stone in the garden. When we rebuilt it and made it bigger, we used Irish limestone. However, if I couldn't afford proper stone (and we are still paying off the overdraft for the last lot of paving) I would quite like concrete, providing it was in large enough slabs, well put down and not pretending to be real stone. (Concrete that completely fools you to begin with is intensely irritating, as it looks just like real stone, until you notice the pattern repeating itself.) Lastly, always make your outdoor sitting area much bigger than you thought it should be in the first place: if it looks too big, you can quickly make it look smaller by adding groups of pots or a series of pots set out in a row like a moveable hedge.

We'll hover briefly over the subject of structural plants. I love big in-your-face plants with loads of shape: plants such as artichokes with great silver feathers for leaves, the largest hostas ('Sum and Substance', 'Snowden'), *Astelia chathamica*, (90cm/3ft), the tender ricepaper plant, *Tetrapanax papyrifer* (3m/10ft) and the magnificent but viciously spiny biennial scotch thistle *Onopordum acanthium* (2m/7ft). If, next time you go out into your garden, you think a particular planting area is looking a bit weak, with many flimsy plants, try adding some of these for a bit of oomph. You can add very important evergreen structure by planting columnar plants such as clipped yews or, in mild climates, Italian cypress (*Cupressus sempervirens*, 40m/130ft). A note about yews: Graham Stuart Thomas, the famous rosarian and gardens/plant adviser to the National Trust for many years, told me that you must use English yew (*Taxus baccata,* 15m/50ft) for making a good clipped slender column. The Irish yew (*T. baccata* 'Fastigiata', 6m/20ft), a form discovered growing in Northern Ireland that is naturally sticky-uppy in shape, doesn't work nearly so well, for it (like us all) becomes fatter and fatter with advancing years. I took out two this autumn. To slim your Irish yews down, cut away every second of the outside branches, and on no account take out the centre of the tree. (If you do, there'll be nothing to tie the remaining outer branches to.)

Man-made structures such as pergolas, summerhouses, tunnels of arches, single arches, metal or wooden poles, obelisks and so on are especially telling structures for the garden because their height doesn't vary from the day you install them. But although they can be terrifically valuable additions, be careful not to commit the easy mistake of installing too many.

We are always told that the very first thing we must do on getting a garden is to make a plan. In fact I once had to write a very long chapter on the subject – thirty pages of it to be precise – in a book called *The Flower Garden* (one of the Royal Horticultural Society Collection, Conran Octopus, 1993). 'Whatever your starting point,' I announced, '. . . good planning is needed at the outset.' A perfectly good book it was, with excellent advice, the received wisdom of hundreds of years. But, in fact, the last thing I ever want do is to make a plan – I feel weak just thinking about it. 'Working with what you have' was one of the headings. Quite. But when we arrived at this garden thirty-six years ago I took no notice of the fact that the soil was light, dry and limey. I ordered rhododendrons, acers, magnolias, meconopsis and choice woodland plants in abundance. The 70cm/28in of Dublin rainfall was neither here nor there; parcels arrived with rheums, rodgersias, gunneras, bog primulas and astilbes. My idea of heaven was (and still is) to indulge in a lavish buying spree. And the consequences? Too bad. Bugger plans.

Clipped hornbeam, trained to arches, at Dan Hinkley and Robert Jones's former home at Heronswood Nursery, near Seattle

Sitting in the garden

'Do you ever sit down in the garden?' 'Not much,' is the somewhat ratty answer. No sooner have I sat down than I see something that needs doing. Off I go for the secateurs or whatever. The deadhead or weed removed, down again I sit. Nagging little reminders soon come trotting along. What about that thistle? I'd better get up and deal with it. And another thing: did the beans get watered last night? Gardening never glides to a peaceful stop; it's a vocation that rolls endlessly on.

No. During the day I probably don't sit down much. But there are other times when I do – in the early morning or just before it gets dark, and especially on a mild winter day when everything's quiet. In these dreamy sort of times I can breathe. The garden's full of calm, a place to revive in. I sit really still and screw up my eyes so that the sun's rays are turned into tiny bright sparks of light, filtered through my eyelashes, against the blue of the sky. I find that light is the most thrilling component of being in a garden. You can make a garden that's full of rare plants, subtle colour schemes and audacious design, and still these would add up to only 50 per cent of the beauty. Light is the other half. I love what it does. And I adore sitting and staring at the sky and watching the cloudscapes and sunshowers go by. (A sunshower is when it rains but the sun still shines through, so the shower doesn't last long.) However small your garden, you can still have your own piece of sky. Nobody can take that away. All you need is an old kitchen chair or a large bucket turned upside down to sit on.

Seats are not only useful for sitting down on, signifying repose. They are something to focus on at the end of a view or path, drawing the eye as would a statue or urn. I like discovering hidden corners on garden visits, perhaps with two small chairs and a table, suggesting conversation and drinks. (It could be that the chat and the drinks never actually take place, but the idea is soothing.) When you first buy a seat for the garden, try it out in several positions. Also, it's probably best set on a piece of paving – if a seat is set on gravel or lawn the legs are always shifting and never stay level.

Your main sitting area is probably made of stone. Don't make the mistake that we did of power hosing it to remove algae: I never

Dianella caerulea var. *petasmodes* growing near nineteenth-century cast-iron chairs

realized how soft stone can be and using the power hose, even once or twice, has gouged out very obvious little holes in the Irish limestone behind the house and, sadly, in the *circa* 1830 granite of the front steps. I used to scrub these by hand with a stiff brush but was tempted by the ease of power hosing. The algae have returned with relish.

Paths

The paths in our garden are made of bricks, old sandstone, new sandstone, old granite, Chinese granite, cobbles, cement slabs, gravel, Irish limestone, pebble mosaic and small areas (relicts of naff days of the 1970s) of crazy paving – in fact any old bit of stone that happened to come in handy at the time. To walk along the paths that we laid when we first came is like reading an old diary: fragments of the past present themselves unasked.

Someone, probably in the 1960s, had a brainwave about garden design with mostly catastrophic results: the idea involved a hosepipe, or possibly more than one, which was to be allowed to drape itself gracefully around your garden wherever it happened to arrange its curvaceous plastic self. You then, following its supposedly gracious line, positioned your paths or cut the shape of flowerbeds in the lawn, and lo! the reshaping of your garden was done. I've never reckoned that hosepipes come with great artistic instinct and suspect that many of the more wiggly kinds of path you see in older gardens are the direct result of design by hosepipe. Even William Robinson (who believed Nature herself should be the only true model for garden design) remarked in *The English Flower Garden*, 'A straight line is often the most beautiful that can be used.' I love straight lines, but still, thirty-six years ago when we first arrived I couldn't wait to put curves in all the straight paths . . . (to my shame I notice that I myself recommended – in print – using a hosepipe for shaping flowerbeds, in *The Flower Garden*).

Ideally, they say, paths should be wide enough for two people to walk abreast in comfort. I totally agree, except I find it difficult to do myself, not wanting to relinquish so much growing space. But I have managed it in some areas, such as the paving alongside the canal in the centre of the garden.

Two paths in particular here at Sandford Road have made quite a dramatic difference, not so much from a design point of view but for reasons of access. Both are near boundary walls, so the growing conditions are overshadowed and dryish anyway and the ground might just as well be used for paths. We can now easily reach any of the climbers and wall shrubs if they need dealing with. I find that positions for plants at

Candytuft, *Verbascum* 'Frosted Gold', linaria and *Centranthus ruber* 'Albus' growing in the dry bed near the cement slab path which was one of the first we put in.

Candytuft, *Verbascum* 'Frosted Gold', alstroemerias and white valerian growing in the same bed. The soil here is very dry and over-used — it was first planted more than a hundred years ago. But these dear good plants thrive.

the path edge are particularly valuable: plants can get the space they need to flourish and you, the gardener, can get right up close to deal with them. Many times when I'm wandering around the garden trying to decide where to position a plant, I ask myself how much attention it needs. If it has to be regularly staked, watered and deadheaded, then it must be under one's nose, whereas a plant such as a Japanese anemone (*Anemone* x *hybrida*, 1.5m/5ft) needs just two minutes in late autumn for a cut back, so it can be planted in a relatively inaccessible position.

We are now planting delphiniums (which seem to spend their entire growing season in intensive care) right beside the paths. If you can have direct, paved access to the back of beds, rather than having to blunder through the beds, making footprints that must be forked up and muddy shoes that'll have to be scraped, a whole new planting area will evolve. You can have a nice spring walk with early bulbs planted near the path for you to enjoy, and their dying leaves in early summer will be hidden by later-flowering plants.

There are two ways in particular of enjoying a garden. One is by looking at the overall picture, as one great eyeful. Great sweeps of colour blend into each other and you don't notice individual flowers. The other way is to walk slowly round having a close look at the singular beauty of

each plant. For close examination you need lots of paths.

Although I haven't got any myself, I love grass paths, particularly those with daisies

Eryngium x *oliverianum* and delphiniums in the bed on the other side of the path. The soil here is less exhausted (this part of the garden was lawn until our day), and the position is more open, so it suits fussier plants.

growing in them. If we hadn't already got rid of both lawns, I'd just let the grass grow tall and only mow wide paths through them. I can't imagine a better way of saving work: giving up mown grass and letting wild flowers grow.

Lastly, a small rant about stepping stones. They work in flowerbeds for extra access provided you keep them swept. They don't work set in lawn, because the edging of each slab's surrounding grass makes lots more work, and it rarely gets done properly. Stepping stones set in gravel are the worst (unless they are standing proud of the gravel), because the small pebbles that make the gravel stick to any passing shoe are transported around the garden. Gravel has an instinct to be always on the move; it's been shifting around the planet since the last Ice Age and it doesn't intend to stop.

Difficult shade

'I've got shade,' said this woman, in a low voice, as if she was announcing an attack of diarrhoea. Well, we all have shade, but there are multiple sorts of shade, from dust-dry positions inhospitable to plants to sheltered places where the soil is always moist and there's a self-perpetuating mulch of leafmould from nearby trees.

It's easier if you know right from the beginning that you can't grow anything at all directly underneath conifers or a hedge of x *Cupressocyparis leylandii*. Even near such a hedge, plants will find the going very challenging. Under mature deciduous trees, such as beech and horse chestnut, snowdrops will manage, and out towards the edge of the tree shadow many more bulbs will finish their growth cycle before the trees comes into leaf.

When you first get possession of a garden it takes time to learn which shady areas are benevolently disposed towards plants and where the soil doesn't dry out in summer, as opposed to places that look nicely damp in spring but soon become rock hard. 'I don't care – I'll water it,' you say. But by midsummer there'll be far too much else happening, all the newly planted summer stuff will demand attention and it'll be bye-bye plant. Some time in late autumn you'll suddenly remember it. You will identify the spot where it was originally interred. A pang of guilt, and then you'll forget all about it. Until the next victim.

North walls need some qualification. They might be on the shady side of a tall apartment block, in which case your plant list is limited. Or you have a north-facing garden wall that's only 1.8m/6ft high. Here, at the foot, provided it isn't overshadowed, it will be bright in summer and you'll have much more scope.

One of my pet small evergreen shrubs, sarcococca or sweet box, does brilliantly in dry shade. I have several, including *S. hookeriana* var. *digyna* (1.8m/6ft), but they are all good. Even in dismal corners their glossy leaves look happy. On a mild day in early spring, if you're anywhere near a bush, you seem to walk through a great waft of scent. If you go back to work out where it's coming from, it probably will have disappeared.

Japanese anemones take a long time to establish but are excellent shade plants.

A classic dry shade plant is *Euphorbia amygdaloides* var. *robbiae* (85cm/33in). Its long-lasting lime-green flowers are offset by dark evergreen leaves. It's a great colonizer – just what you want in unfavourable conditions. I like it a lot. People sometimes complain to me that it's difficult to get rid of. Well, you can't have it both ways: this plant is prepared to colonize and prosper. But, about the end of June, when there are a million distractions, you must cut back the faded flower stems to the base. Many people (myself included) are allergic to the white sap.

You may sniff at the inclusion of *Euonymus fortunei* 'Emerald Gaiety' (90cm/3ft), 'Emerald 'n' Gold' and their relations. Not exactly the smartest plants on the roundabout (but I'd rather have a live chav than a dead duchess), these euonymus are stalwarts of the reliable small evergreen shrub department, with cheerful dispositions, flashy variegated leaves and a constitution that will thrive where most plants would give up.

Brunnera macrophylla 'Langtrees' (60cm/2ft) is a borage relation with heart-shaped hairy leaves of little interest to slugs and blue forget-me-not flowers in spring. My plant has been excellent in dry shade. It came from Beth Chatto's nursery nearly a quarter of a century ago, and the foliage is heavily spotted in silver. You see many poor examples of this cultivar around, with hardly any spots – obviously not the true plant. I think it a better plant than *B.m.* 'Dawson's White' and 'Hadspen Cream', both of which have good variegated leaves but scorch at the edges if put under stress in summer. Even the beautiful veined and silvered foliage of the much-trumpeted 'Jack Frost' throws a huge sulk in too dry a summer.

And then there's the incomparable Japanese anemone (*Anemone* x *hybrida*, 1.5m/5ft), an excellent long-term dry shade plant – but it may take a few years to establish. The native male fern *Dryopteris filix-mas* (90cm/3ft) will live happily in a dry position without complaint, whereas most ferns demand a better, moister spot. Foxgloves (*Digitalis purpurea*) will take dryness at the root but don't like total gloom. You can make lovely evergreen dry-shade-tolerant carpets out of London pride (*Saxifraga* x *urbium*, 15cm/6in). Just keep dividing the plants into different rosettes and replant them. I can't do this any more myself because in our garden vine weevils scoff up all members of the saxifrage family with gusto.

Hellebores, of course, prefer shade, but the only one that I'd recommend with confidence for dry shade would be *Helleborus foetidus* (80cm/32in), the black-green deeply fingered leaves of which beautifully compliment the lime-green clusters of bell-shaped flowers. *Iris foetidissima* (90cm/3ft), another so-called smelly plant (although I can't get the smell factor of either), has beautiful clean evergreen leaves, unexciting flowers and long-lasting heads of shiny red seeds. A group of this looks good. *Acanthus mollis* (90cm/3ft) and the grass *Luzula sylvatica* (80cm/32in) are sometimes recommended for dry shade, but in both cases here they became so infected with mildew that I had to move them to better positions. The small tuber *Arum italicum* subsp. *italicum* 'Marmoratum' (formerly *Arum italicum* 'Pictum', 45cm/18in) times its growth to suit our winter gardens. The shining bright-green marbled leaves emerge in autumn and look sparkling fresh all winter. They are lovely to mix with a bunch of supermarket daffodils.

A plant that's no great beauty (boring leaves) but has a delicious scent is the perennial honesty (*Lunaria rediviva*, 75cm/30in). This was recommended to me first by Professor John Malins, the late husband of the garden writer and designer Penelope Hobhouse, a charming and knowledgeable man. Both this and the biennial honesty or silver dollar plant (*Lunaria annua*, 90cm/3ft) are major contenders for the excellence-in-dry-shade medal. Both have unremarkable leaves and silvery satin see-through seedheads, rounded in the biennial and more elliptical in the perennial. For use in the house, harvest as the pods turn brown, hang them up to dry and allow the outsides of the pods to fall away. You have to move around the seedlings of biennial honesty to where you want them for the following year, whereas the perennial will potter on indefinitely in the same place, self-seeding as well. I have some tucked away beside the front door and others are growing underneath the Californian tree poppy (*Romneya coulteri*, 2.5m/8ft), so you can't see them, but their fragrance is undiminished.

Other plants you could try in dry shade: *Cyclamen coum* and *C. hederifolium*; bluebells (*Hyacinthoides non-scripta*); *Vinca minor*; *Geranium phaeum* 'Album' and *G. macrorrhizum;* and brilliant, easy-going and very tolerant *Polystichum setiferum* cultivars.

A friend of mine, Rose Mary O'Brien, in a garden up the road where we live, at number 49, has made brilliant use of an inhospitable space under an enormous evergreen oak (probably the finest evergreen tree for our climate). This example of the holm oak (*Quercus ilex*, 21m/70ft) is as tall as a three-storey building and forms a great mass of dark and sombre green, casting a heavy shade. Most of us would have attempted to grow periwinkles and other shade-tolerant plants beneath it. She has spread the whole area of shade beneath the tree with gravel and arranged fourteen very large terracotta pots in a straight row following the garden wall. Each pot contains a mature camellia. The shining dark green leaves of these shrubs, some of which are up to thirty years old, are testament to perfect health and every plant is a mass of blossom in spring. The holm oak, together with the row of large camellias, gives a wonderful, formal Italianate air to the garden.

I am always asking Rose Mary why she is so successful with her camellias. Apparently she keeps the pots permanently moist and feeds the plants with liquid ericaceous fertilizer unfailingly once a week from mid-June until the end of August. Now she is starting another row of large pots, in this case with hydrangeas. Both these and the camellias make marvellous long-term container plants, but they are extremely dependent on you or your watering system.

Choice shade

Gardeners are always contrary. If we live in shady gardens there's nothing we want more than South African and Mediterranean plants. If we live in dry gardens, as I do, there's nothing we want more than choice American woodland plants. I want to grow bloodroots and trilliums and podophyllums more than anything. I do grow them, and they are getting by, but I'd be a more relaxed gardener if I didn't always want the unsuitable. I grow most of these special plants in shady raised beds, where I've worked lots of peat into the existing soil.

In March visitors are always stopped in their tracks by the sight of my best clump of trilliums, *T. chloropetalum* (50cm/30in) with satiny deep crimson-petalled flowers atop green and maroon mottled leaves. The clump (I bought the first plant in the late 1970s) has expanded with extreme sloth and, after suffering several name changes, is growing in the best kind of shade, at the foot of a 3m/10ft north-facing stone wall. In no way is the position threatened by nearby wandering roots or the dreaded overhang of coniferous trees. Trillium snouts are vulnerable from late autumn on, when, secreted under fallen leaves, their luscious little noses may be trodden on, to dire effect. In many ways their greatest enemy is either me or one of the dogs, Mr Reginald and Daisy, rushing by on the scent of a cat. Thus a low green wire fence surrounds the clump. A good tip for encouraging trilliums to bulk up is to give them a weekly feed of potash-rich tomato fertilizer from the beginning of March to the end of May, and to copy the conditions in their native North American woodlands by offering them a mulch of leafmould, preferably oak or beech. *Trillium rivale* is a lovely small trillium (7cm/3in) growing near by; it is also good in a trough.

If you ever cut the root of Canadian bloodroot (*Sanguinaria canadensis*, 30cm/12in), you'll see why it is so called. The roots produce a bloody sap. Dr Molly Sanderson, the Northern Irish gardener after whom the famous black viola was named, gave me the beautiful double form and told me to divide it only when it is in growth (spring), and not to plant the roots too deeply. I once had the delectable pink form, another plant that should have been surrounded by an anti-disturbance device. The leaves of the bloodroot are blue-grey with a powdery blue reverse. Himalayan *Podophyllum hexandrum* (45cm/18in), which has lovely blotched brownish leaves and

Trillium rivale makes a good trough plant for shade.

pink fleeting flowers, is still extant. To lose one of the very special *Podophyllum* given to me as *P. versipelle* may be regarded as a misfortune; to lose two looks like carelessness. Both mine had whopping, hexagonal satiny leaves, which the slugs used to practise gliding on. They get the blame, anyway.

Kirengeshoma palmata (1.2m/4ft) from Japan likes cool conditions (not easy to find here). It's a distinguished-looking plant with maple-like leaves and fat-petalled flowers in the expensive yellow you see on silk curtains in Eaton Square, on 90cm/3ft stems that look as though they're just about to open properly but never actually do. Enjoying similar conditions are translucent lavender *Thalictrum delavayi* 'Hewitt's Double' (1.2m/4ft) and *T. diffusiflorum* (90cm/3ft), which has large individual flowers that are an entrancing pale blue. I've actually given up on both, but if you've got a cool summer, acid soil, high rainfall and a bottomless source of leafmould you must try them. I find *Actaea* (formerly *Cimicifuga*) *simplex* Atropurpurea Group (90cm/3ft) much more tolerant of warmth and drier conditions. It gives you good clean divided dusky purple foliage all season and slender spires of autumn blossom with a hauntingly sweet perfume that seems to say, 'This is the end of summer – enjoy.'

There are many plants that I would categorize in neither 'difficult shade' nor 'choice shade' – easy plants such as Solomon's seal, lily-of-the-valley, most hellebores, smilacina, omphalodes, pulmonaria, *Alchemilla mollis* (45cm/18in) uvularia, liriope, tellima, bergenia, arisaema, aspidistra, asarum, lamium, epimedium, heuchera and so on.

Before deciding where to plant something, just ask yourself, 'What sort of shade do I have?'

Watering

I often imagine meetings organized by manufacturers of garden tools. Earnest young men wearing black have stimulating discussions concerning the design of handles. But when the subject of the meeting concerns the design of the spout of a watering can, I suspect it's all about style and nothing to do with pouring ability (let alone colour, often a sickly pale green). The resulting cans cause water to gush out all at once with a hiccuppy gurgle, like a bad teapot. As a result seedlings lose their tenuous hold on life and even established pot plants lose the top half-inch of soil.

To me there is only one watering can worth having, and that's one made by Haws. It has perfect balance for lugging up and down the garden, and when you use the rose (metal thing with little holes in) the plants receive a gentle spray, like a benediction of summer rain.

Having water available on tap in various spots around the garden means that you don't put off watering something that needs it. In classic Edwardian gardens Edwin Lutyens had the sensible idea of providing dipping wells. We have placed large wooden barrels or dustbins under our taps as it's quicker to dunk a watering can than wait for it to fill from the tap.

The most soothing job in the garden is to stand, on a warm evening, holding a garden hose, aiming the water absentmindedly at no plant in particular. It gives a satisfying feeling of hard work when it's nothing of the sort. I reckon it's the lazy sprinkle that probably harms the plants, by encouraging roots towards the surface, and it's better gardening to give each plant an occasional really good soak with a can. Plants in this garden that are watered very regularly by hand on summer evenings are clematis, delphiniums and dahlias. Each has a whole can – 6.8 litres/1½ gallons. I once read that it was a good idea to sink an upended drainpipe beside plants that need watering often, so that when you aim the spout of the can at the pipe you can be sure water's getting straight to the roots. Taking this idea a step further, I sink pots (2.25 litres/½ gallon) into the ground near wall shrubs, with their rim at soil level. In spring, lots of large tender plants, such as salvias, also in half-gallon pots, need hardening off in a sheltered place outside, and are inclined to fall over, as they are top heavy. I anchor their pots within the sunken pots. I later remove the tender potted stuff and plant it out. All summer we water the plants in the notoriously dry wall beds via the sunken pots. Otherwise the water just runs, instead of sinking in.

An easy trap for beginners concerns the watering of containers. How many times have I heard people say that there's been rain, and therefore there's no need to water? Probably all the rain has done is make the leaves look satisfyingly damp, leaving the roots dry (incidentally an invitation to mildew). Even in winter (not in frosty weather) established evergreens in pots, such as camellias, bay trees and box, need watering. In summer containers need an immense amount of water, certainly once a day and possibly twice when it's hot. A whole watering can per large pot is the ration. You often hear it said that watering should not be done when the sun is out, because the drops of water act like magnifying glasses and can burn the foliage. I saw this happen once, when a rodgersia was scorched. But I'd rather see the odd frizzled leaf than see plants short of water.

Watering under glass needs special care. Remember that apprentice gardeners in the eighteenth and nineteenth centuries had to have seven years' experience before being allowed to water in the greenhouse. Under glass in winter be very careful about watering when growth is at a standstill. By splashing water around you'll encourage grey mould (*Botrytis*), a fungus that thrives in close, damp conditions. In our greenhouse this disease turns up unfailingly every December, however fastidious I am about picking off dead leaves, tidying up and not leaving leaf litter around. Plants that are resting (pelargoniums and fuchsias, for example) cannot absorb excess water and may need watering once a week or less, whereas young plants, such as autumn-rooted cuttings, should be kept just damp. Also, it depends on the temperature of the greenhouse how much water you give. The colder you keep the greenhouse, the less you should water. (The water itself should be the same temperature as the greenhouse.) If a plant is overwatered it looks miserable, water doesn't seem to revive it and the pot is too heavy. Probably the last few times you noticed the plant it was limp, so you gave it another slosh, thus ensuring death by overwatering (a remarkably common occurrence).

In summer under glass you should have an entirely different approach. Even when in a hurry before leaving for work, make sure to remember to open the ventilation. The temperature can soar quickly when the sun's out and trays of seedlings can shrivel fast if allowed to dry out. Damp down the floor, which means slosh water all over it several times a day. This makes more humidity and less of an invitation to red spider, a pest that thrives on dry air, and cools the greenhouse down temporarily. An interesting phenomenon is that on warm days in spring and autumn, by damping down the greenhouse in late afternoon, say four o'clock, and then shutting all doors and all ventilation, the climate inside becomes deliciously warm and beneficial to plant growth.

I think grouping all the plants that need extra watering in the same place is a valuable concept. It saves you from dashing here and there to rescue a fainting phlox, willow gentian (*Gentiana asclepiadea*, 60cm/24in) or astilbe.

Seeds

It's an exhilarating moment when the first tray of seeds you've ever sown germinate. There they are, dear little things, all 150 of them. How could you possibly part with any? But in order for a few to thrive, you must cull about 130. Otherwise you risk losing the lot to what's known as damping off, when a fungus causes a few of them to go funny looking and collapse, rapidly followed by the rest. As an additional precaution, when sowing seed avoid overcrowding and be sure to use clean seed trays and sterilized seed compost. Beware of sowing seeds of tender plants too early in the year; later, when it's warmer, you can get them out of the house quickly.

To sow seed, unless I have a packet of a hardy annual (such as nasturtiums, English marigolds or opium poppies) to be sown directly into open ground, this is what I do. Fill a small pot (8cm/3in) or small seed tray with fresh seed compost and gently firm the compost so that it is within 1cm/½in of the top. Water, using a fine rose. Let it drain. Especially with very fine seeds, I like to water before sowing so that they don't get washed away. Sow seed very thinly. Sieve a little compost over them – an old kitchen sieve is useful for this. Label.

Then there are three different possibilities:

(a) Cover the pot with grit and leave it in a cool place outside. Plants native to temperate regions often need a period of freezing weather (as they would have had in the wild) to encourage germination, which could take months, even years in some cases. The grit is to help to prevent mosses and liverworts. With seeds that could take a year or more to germinate I don't like using soilless composts because they can become compacted. I prefer to make a mix of a third each of good soil, peat or leafmould and sharp grit (see page 37).

(b) Put the pot into a polythene bag. Seal. Place in an airing cupboard or hot press (the Irish term). This suits half-hardy annuals – cosmos, tobacco plants (*Nicotiana*) and runner beans (one or two seeds per pot), for example.

(c) Cover the pot with a sheet of glass or perspex. Lay several sheets of newspaper on top. Put in greenhouse. Turn over the glass every day and wipe off condensation (another cause of damping off).

Often I try all three methods. The moment germination happens, move the seedlings to a light position.

This is when the trouble really begins. Not everybody has a greenhouse. Conservatories are light-filled house extensions to suit people rather than plants. You need a light windowsill in a room that's not too warm, where the temperature doesn't fluctuate too much. Otherwise seedlings become etiolated – that is, all drawn up and pale through want of light.

The next step requires more space. You must prick out the best of the

Cornflowers (*Centaurea cyanus*)

seedlings. This means very gingerly easing something like a label underneath the chosen seedling and then picking it up – not by the stem, which you could squash by mistake, but by one of its leaves. (It's like trying to explain how to handle babies or puppies.) You then make a hole in the seed compost in an individual small pot, by sticking a finger in, and pop in the seedling. You could also set the seedlings about 5cm/2in apart in a tray. I usually settle the potting mix around the roots of the seedling by giving the pot a little tap on the potting bench. You then find another warm, very light place for the young plant to develop. (Note: You'll notice that I've mentioned 'small pot' several times. If you generously choose a larger pot, there'll be so much surplus potting mix that it will become waterlogged and the plant's roots could drown. Another point: exactly how firm the seedling should be is hard to explain. The roots should be in contact with the potting mix but not jammed solid. Usually all gets nicely settled in by watering using a fine spray.)

Soon after this, you should pinch out the seedlings. This means you take out (using scissors or finger and thumb) the nice healthy-looking shoot at the top of the plant. The plant then forms lots of side shoots, ensuring that you don't get a long, thin streak of misery with one flower on top.

Incidentally, it's often no economy to sow stale seed. Every autumn I sow cornflowers so that I've got nice big plants the following spring for filling in after the tulips. I'd heard that the daisy family (the *Asteraceae*), of which the cornflower (*Centaurea cyanus*) is a member, was slow to germinate if the seed was stale. The old seed this year took three weeks to come up, whereas new packets of seed germinated in two days in the hot press.

Potting for beginners

First, I'd like to clear up a confusion that won't go away. It concerns the word 'compost', which means 'mixture'. The same word is used for garden compost (well-rotted vegetable matter) and for the potting compost (which is either soil- or peat-based) that you buy in bags at a garden centre. You can understand why garden novices get muddled. I'm often being told about people using neat garden compost for potting, and the plants are so stuffed with food that they become the vegetable version of a Strasbourg goose.

Peat-based compost is easily available, but not ideal: it becomes too compacted, once it dries out it's hard to wet again (try dunking the pot in a bucket of water and leaving for several hours) and – the most puzzling aspect for beginners, as it looks so wonderfully dark and rich – although it's lovely for roots to explore in their search for nourishment, peat is virtually without nutrients. Plant food is added to the mix in the form of chemicals, but it is usually only programmed to last for about six weeks. And the use of peat itself is questionable. Has it been harvested from a sustainable source?

For long-term container plants such as roses and hydrangeas, large pots with perennial herbs and sinks for alpines (anything other than annuals), I'd rather use a soil-based compost. Good topsoil is as hard to describe as it is to find a reputable source. Old books mention loam. This was traditionally prepared by stacking up turf in neat piles and then sterilizing it. If you ever remove a lawn, as we did, you'll have a good supply of topsoil. In an ideal world it should be sterilized. I make a mixture of roughly one third each of nice crumbly topsoil, peat or leafmould and sharp grit.

I've sieved leafmould all my life, rubbing it through an old-fashioned wire-and-wood sieve. The best leafmould is crumbly, brown and rich in humus. You find it just under the leaves that fell the previous autumn. Oak or beech leaves are the best, and don't include sycamore, leathery evergreens or pine needles. To make your own leafmould, either stack up autumn leaves in a wire-netting enclosure or fill large polythene sacks with

We put fifty to eighty tulips in each dustbin, planted in about eight different layers. Whatever depth you plant them, they come up and flower as usual.

leaves, charge at them several times with a garden fork to make air holes (thinking of your enemies meanwhile) and forget about it for a year.

You need grit in a potting mix to help it drain properly. Good sharp grit will 'talk' to you – squeeze it in your hand and it will make a complaining, scrunchy noise. Much of the grit I've been buying recently is too claggy and clogged up with muddy particles. You must rinse it many times through a fine sieve or else it'll be no use for improving drainage.

Terracotta or plastic? Apart from the aesthetic consideration the big difference is in the drainage. A plastic pot filled with peat-based compost shouldn't need any drainage material in the bottom, whereas a terracotta, metal or carved stone pot, with perhaps only one drainage hole, needs to be prepared so that it doesn't get blocked. Lay crocks, or bits of broken flowerpot, over the hole, curved side up, or convex like the vault of heaven (bits of brick smashed with a hammer would do if you haven't any crocks). Add plenty more, and then put a layer of gravel before your potting mix. A large container needs 10cm/4in of drainage and something like an old dustbin, one of my favourite containers, needs about 30cm/12in.

If you are repotting for the first time, when the roots are crowding the pot, here's how to do it. Pick up the plant with your right hand; put your left hand near the rim of the pot at soil level, and, pressing against the soil, hold the middle of the plant steady between the outstretched first and second fingers. With one movement, still holding the pot in two places, turn it upside down and give the rim a little tap on the potting bench. The plant, roots nicely anchored by the soil (otherwise it didn't need repotting in the first place), should fall out cleanly, as you hold it with your left hand. Reverse it neatly into the new, larger pot (but not too large – see page 35), in which you have already placed a handful or so of potting mix. Keep filling the pot up and tapping it several times on the bench to settle things. It's most important to insert the plant at exactly the same level as it was originally: too deep, and it could rot at the base. Firm gently (I love this – a complete contradiction, neatly covering the writer in case the plant doesn't grow, like another well-used gardening term, 'moist but well drained'). Finally, water, using a fine rose.

An important point: in winter, unless you can offer them the protection of a frame or greenhouse, plants are far more vulnerable to cold, wet weather when potted than when they are planted out. Just test the different temperatures by sticking your finger in open ground and then in the pot and you'll see why. If you have to leave potted plants outside, tuck them under a warm wall, and with something like lilies turn the pots on their sides for the coldest months to keep the compost fairly dry.

Planting

Where to plant something is the most important decision of all. The position the plant would prefer takes priority over where I think it would look good. Sun or shade? Dry or damp? Woodland or meadow? Clay or sandy soil? Or perhaps it's a common old English garden plant, such as the perennial cornflower (*Centaurea montana*, 90cm/3ft), which nobody mentions and which isn't fussy at all. I spend hours walking round in circles trying to decide where to plant. I often end up taking the plant back to base beside the potting shed. It could be that the more you know about gardening, the more complicated it becomes. I envy the novice gardener – old hands are too aware of pitfalls. On first seeing an adult vine weevil, whose young are yobbish, munching white grubs, I said to myself, 'Innocent small black beetle,' and, decades ago, oblivious to the dangers of honey fungus, I noticed some toadstools. I looked down and thought, 'Lovely. How romantic!' I had no idea that this widespread – in old Dublin gardens at any rate – fungus attacks and destroys many woody plants.

How much competition a plant will stand is of serious interest. Some meadow plants are prepared to fight their way towards the light. The big tribe of American daisies, for example, such as helianthus, heliopsis, heleniums and silphiums, are used to roughing it out on the prairie. Other plants, such as *Cirsium rivulare* (1.2m/4ft), a moisture-loving, burgundy thistle, or pale blue scabious-like *Knautia arvensis* (1.5m/5ft) and *Hedysarum coronarium* (1m/3ft), which looks like the queen of all the clovers, have tallish flower stems but basal foliage that dislikes being shaded out by neighbouring plants. So, if you put them towards the back of a bed, as their flowering height would suggest, they cannot cope, as their leaves don't get enough sunlight. So I am constantly adding to lists in my head entitled 'Competition' and 'Must have isolation', and I never stop readjusting the planting. Newcomers to gardening seem to think that you get the garden 'done' and, as with your new kitchen or bathroom, that's it – you admire the makeover, and from then on it looks after itself. But gardens are never completely right, and perhaps the allure of the garden is that it's never, ever right.

When to plant is up for discussion. I make some of my best decisions in summer. I can see then where there is a real space. In spring what looks empty is nothing of the sort: I forget that some whopping clump of *Eupatorium purpureum* subsp. *maculatum* 'Atropurpureum' (2m/7ft), Joe Pye weed, will totally overshadow it. Even with a hundred gardening books, and the ghost of Gertrude Jekyll whispering information in my ear, it's hard to judge the height, and especially the bulk, of a plant. I often position tall grasses, such as miscanthus, still in their pots, in late summer when I can see exactly what effect a high fountain of foliage will do to a border. And I do a lot of plonking down of a plant and going back to the house to see what it looks like from there.

Driving along, I've often noticed a method of planting common to landscapers, the 'slice and stamp'. In Ireland this is done with a long-handled spade, sliced at speed into the soil at an angle of forty-five degrees. A spadeful of soil is thrown off to one side. A small tree is chucked into the resulting hole. Soil is scraped over it. The heel of a heavy boot stamps the lot into the ground. I can hardly bear to watch.

I daresay that despite this cavalier method most plants survive, although they may be slow to recover from so miserable a start. In this garden, planting rations are usually a big black bucket of what I hope is a nourishing mix of garden compost, leafmould, bonemeal, topsoil and grit in varying proportions, with added handfuls of pelleted chicken manure. (It could be that making such an effort makes me feel better and makes no difference whatsoever to the plant. And it could even be that the sooner plants adapt to the poorish, overgardened soil here, the better.)

To wobble another of the hard-core gardening rules: I've always insisted on the value of digging a really big hole. Of course it should be large enough to accommodate the roots, and I still cringe when I see somebody checking the width of the pot of the subject for interment and then digging a mean little hole exactly the same size. But there again, perhaps the plant will adjust more quickly if it doesn't have a wonderful start of a rich and delicious pie. I'm also told, and this has been scientifically proved, that the shape of the modern planting hole should be square, not round. Apparently, many container-grown plants have their roots wrapped round in circles within the pot. When you plant, the roots continue in the same mode and don't bother to explore fresh soil. Whereas if you prepare a square hole, the roots are tempted to investigate and move out towards the corners. The plant thrives as a result.

So, having dug your reasonably sized, possibly square hole, check your plant's roots. If they are dry, soak the still-potted plant for half an hour in a bucket of water. Then remove plant from pot. If the roots are congested, your plant will have a better chance if you tweak them with a kitchen fork, gently teasing away some of the potting mix. If the rootball is very potbound, I sometimes slice off the bottom third of the roots with a sharp knife to encourage more roots. Loosen up the soil at the bottom of the hole and add well-rotted garden compost, pelleted chicken manure, whatever you fancy (maybe nothing – apparently the new thinking is that trees should never be fed, not even when first planted; they just have to get on with what's there). Then insert the plant, making sure that, when you have firmed it in, it is at exactly the same soil level as it was before; a

handful of extra soil around the stem of a woody plant, for example, could rot the bark and kill it. If planting something woody, such as a rose or shrub, tread around the plant to firm it in. Little plants just need firm fingers.

Heleniums are classic ingredients of the herbaceous border. As they're used to toughing it out on the prairie, they will do well in most conditions, provided the soil is not too dry. Rosy-red *Phygelius capensis* can be grown as a shrub or cut down each spring to ground level and treated as a herbaceous plant.

Even if it's raining, water your plant in. This settles the soil nicely around the roots. Many people use a mulch of a loose layer of organic material to prevent evaporation around a newly planted plant. I'm happy with a mulch of garden compost, but wary of some of the bark available. If fresh and resinous smelling, it could harm the plant.

Feeding

All my gardening life I've lauded the benefits of farmyard manure. Brilliant stuff. Until the advent of garden chemicals, manure was just about the only soil conditioner and plant food anyway. But recently I've begun to worry about its content. I suspect (a totally unscientific comment) that chemicals I don't know about lurk therein. Weedkiller residue from the straw, perhaps? Insecticide and fungicide sprayed on the original crop? Antibiotics injected into the cattle that stood on the straw? Also, it could be that, having used it on this garden for thirty-five years, I've brought about an imbalance of nutrients. I remember, in the 1980s, the head of a horticultural research station here in Ireland warned me that old gardens (such as this) that have been cultivated for generations can have a build-up of phosphates caused by constant use of farmyard manure. Sometimes I think I can hear my plants saying, 'Easy on the manure.'

Just to mention compost seems to put a spell on people, even if they're not interested in gardening. Opinions about how to make it are discussed at dinner parties. People pontificate. Despite being a fashion statement, the compost heap is undeniably the heart of the garden, the place where unwanted garden waste and kitchen vegetable trimmings are transformed into a crumbly, brown, pleasant-smelling material. Rotted vegetable matter (known in gardening books as humus) added to the soil enables roots to move through smoothly, gathering nutrients.

Our compost heaps (you need two: one that you're making and one that you're using, full of ripe compost) are built out of cement blocks, with lots of wide gaps for ventilation. In front they have supports for wooden slats that are slotted in, to stop everything falling out. As the heap rises, we add more slats. The roofs are made out of planks covered in roofing felt. You can make excellent compost containers out of wooden pallets, with a bit of carpet on top to keep the warmth in. You can also get proprietary plastic bins, ideal for corners of small gardens.

Compost heaps can range from the *de luxe* five-star sort right down to what is, in effect, a rubbish heap. Even the latter – though the stuff takes longer to rot and you might have to pick out large woody prickly bits and old beer cans – will eventually form a useful supply of humus.

Grass cuttings and leafy green weeds heat up fast, whereas woody stuff like hedge prunings are slow to rot. A combination of the two is what you want, and then the coarse bits aerate the green stuff. Too much of the latter and you get a smelly wodge akin to silage (unless you are making compost in a solid plastic container with no holes, when everything gets hot and smelly without air, but eventually turns into a pile of good stuff just the same).

Soil from weed roots is normally added (we don't, because as in many old gardens the soil here has various fungi in it which I don't wish to circulate via the compost heap). Don't put anything to do with meat on the heap; mother

Ideally you need a couple of compost heaps: one you are still making and a mature heap you are using.

rats like nothing more than a warm compost heap anyway. Don't put on autumn leaves – it's better to make leafmould separately (see page 37). Don't put on lawn mowings if you've recently used weedkiller on the lawn. Don't put on serious weeds such as couch or scutch grass, convolvulus, dandelions or ground elder. We don't use a compost activator. If you get a shredder, it's only worthwhile to get a decent heavy petrol-driven one.

The placement of the compost heaps is most important. When you arrive at a new garden your first instinct, as was mine, is to locate the heaps away at the end of the garden, the position disguised, you hope, by some sort of trellis arrangement, which everybody knows is hiding the compost heap. But you're not going to go down there with a bucket of potato peelings on a dark night. So try to find a location that's both accessible and not noticeable. Preferably you should place compost heaps directly on soil rather than on hard paving.

I can't say enough good things about the addition of compost to the soil, but sometimes a general fertilizer is necessary as well. We don't scatter it all over the beds but give it individually to greedy plants such as clematis, delphiniums, hellebores, dahlias, roses and so on. We usually do this in about March, when the soil is warming up, and again later in the season if plants need it. At the moment our favourite is the organic pelleted chicken manure we also use when planting. When potting, we add Osmacote as we go along, a long-lasting granular balanced fertilizer. We use liquid fertilizer in the greenhouse (once a week in summer) and for containers, and ericaceous liquid fertilizer on plants such as lapageria, rhododendron and camellias. Watering with organic liquid fertilizer has a real feel-good factor, giving you a comforting sense of bounteously caring for your plants.

Weeding

I love the word 'noxious', the traditional description of serious weeds. The leaders of the gang are ground elder, convolvulus, dandelions, brambles, nettles, docks, creeping thistle, the grass known as scutch in Ireland and couch elsewhere, and whatever else is your bag. But it's the sneaky weeds that I've really got it in for. They secrete themselves behind a leaf and, while butter wouldn't melt in their mouths, dedicate themselves to the business of reproduction.

One of the worst is the hairy bittercress (*Cardamine hirsuta*). The moment the soil warms up in spring, up comes a thin stalk with mean flowers in a fetching shade of dirty white. It can set seed fast, ripen it and disperse it by a special shooting method. The cycle continues, with many generations per year. Another monster of the superficially endearing kind is the annual meadow grass (*Poa annua*) – insignificant in appearance but deadly in perseverance. Yet another is a diminutive epilobium – I'm not certain of its name. Curiously, with people, if I don't like somebody, I can't remember his or her name either. The epilobium spends winter disguised as an alpine gem, with a neat rosette of bright green like a baby lily, guaranteed to fool a beginner.

My mentor David Shackleton, the great Irish gardener and plantsman who gardened at Beech Park, County Dublin, and died in 1988, used to say, 'Weeds are a great problem to gardeners. Why grow them?' But I love weeding: it's wonderfully calming. I like being in close contact with my plants and the feeling that, since every weed removed is the potential parent of millions, I'm saving time for the future, when probably all I'll want to do is sit down. Weeding introduces a new perspective on the garden; when you're down at weed level, you get different views, and new ideas come about what plants need dealing with – dividing, say, or watering.

For ground infested with bad weeds, if you don't like using weedkiller, a slower but effective way is to put down sheets of black polythene (or carpet), making sure that the edges are dug in or held down by wooden planks and stones so that no light gets in at the edges. To control horsetail and convolvulus you need to leave this on for a year, or two. Actually, I've a sneaking admiration for all the horsetails (*Equisetum* spp.), ineradicable as they often are: they got here before us, they'll probably survive long after us, and good luck to them. But there's nothing like thorough digging and cleaning if you've got a small space and are dying to get started – you get a terrific feeling of achievement. I reckon any kind of nervous disorder could be cured by the painstaking removal of convolvulus, fat white root by fat white root. I've done it. One area, about 2m/7ft square, took three weeks.

Achilleas, verbascum, apricot *Papaver pilosum* subsp. *spicatum* and self-sown double Welsh poppies

The first weeding of the year here takes place at the start of spring, early February. I work through the beds, tweaking out weeds, riffling up the soil with a small long-handled fork, removing bits of herbaceous clutter. Early summer, when there's a great surge of growth, is an important time to get on top of the weeds. The few that get away now, by hiding under expanding herbaceous plants for example, will drop their seed unnoticed. Out of laziness I like to clean up as I go along – it makes less work – but others like to trample over the bed, gathering weeds, and then tidy it all up later. Incidentally, if you try to pull up a dandelion, it'll invariably break before you get the last bit of taproot out, from which it will regenerate. But if you take time, and carefully rock the plant backwards and forwards for a minute or so, loosening it in the earth, you'll be able, very, very carefully, to pull the whole plant and root clean out.

You could have a good argument about what constitutes a weed. Of course it's 'a plant in the wrong place'. But whereas I go into a sort of trance when weeding, my fingers steering themselves automatically to obvious weeds such as groundsel or chickweed, when it comes to self-sown garden plants such as peach-leaved bellflower (*Campanula persicifolia*, 60cm/2ft), double forms of Welsh poppy (*Meconopsis cambrica*, 60cm/2ft), Mexican daisy (*Erigeron karvinskianus*, 60cm/2ft), pot marigold (*Calendula officinalis*, 30cm/12in) and teasel (*Dipsacus fullonum*, 1.8/6ft), much more concentration is required. I love all these individually, but although they are only seedlings now, is there space for them in future?

Sometimes garden visitors ask, 'How do you get rid of the weeds?' My reply? 'I pick them up between finger and thumb and put them into a bucket.' This is usually followed by silence.

The meanest trick

I'm never quite certain about builders. Nobody ever told me that an estimate is a piece of paper on which figures are constantly adjustable. Nobody ever told me that there is a unique law with regard to that piece of paper: any time after the first week of the job beginning, the figures will shift. But it's when you are a budding gardener, who has at last got their very own garden, that you realize what a mean trick a builder, now so successful that he's become a developer, can play.

The first step in any development is the arrival of a fleet of heavy JCBs. These shift the topsoil up to one end of the site, and either a mountain of it will remain there until the development is completed in two years' time (by which time the soil at the bottom of the pile will have deteriorated by having the air squeezed out of it, and will no longer have the good properties of topsoil), or it is sold off, to topsoil dealers.

When, in another life, I was an antique dealer, I could happily handle any sort of dealer, except the carpet dealers, known as the rug trade, who invariably got the better of me. I'd certainly put topsoil dealers into the same bracket. The only saving grace they have is their presumed ignorance as to exactly what constitutes topsoil. In the nick of time I've managed to turn away deliveries liberally decorated with scutch (or couch) grass, which at least indicates that the soil was from the top. And I once caught a big lorry with its back end ready to drop its load on the pavement outside our house (thus blocking the road and causing ten years of edgy relations with the neighbours). The heap about to descend was a strange pale colour, mixed up with what looked like builders' rubble. The substance was in fact subsoil. (Topsoil is usually darker brown and nice and crumbly looking.)

To get back to the budding gardener and the first garden. The living-room window of the house looks out on to a space surrounded by a wooden fence. The sun beams down. But delight begins to disperse as the new owner notices the surface of the space. There are many puddles, some large footprints already filled with water and a few of what look like reeds. The remainder of the space is a funny sort of lime green. On closer inspection the ground seems to be covered in algae. What has happened?

Possibly this was the area of the development site where the JCBs and other heavy machinery were parked. For two years. Or it could be that this was where concrete mixers arrived every day with ready-mixed concrete, or where the girders were stored, or where the base of one of the giant cranes was installed. As a result, the earth is seriously compressed.

Another, even worse, possibility must be considered. The original drainage of the site – via underground streams, for example – has been irredeemably disturbed, in which case the only remedy is to take advice from an engineer about installing a series of land drains. (Note: If you are concerned about a small area of your garden being badly drained you could dig a soakaway – a 90cm/3ft square hole, filled to three-quarters of its depth with rubble.)

So, not only has all the topsoil been removed but what remains is seriously compacted, sour subsoil. You could try breaking up the ground with a pickaxe, and if the water drains you could import topsoil (remembering the hazards mentioned above). The final resort would be to cover the lot in decking and some large containers. (Of course, if the area is wet throughout the year,

We turned some of my box balls into box bowls.

waterside plants would be happy, but who would want a house leading directly to a bog?)

You meet many young gardeners with similar problems. Even if the subsoil isn't compacted there's the lack of topsoil to contend with. However, whatever soil or lack of it you have, much good can be done by cultivating it (by digging rather than rotovating, which compacts it further) and incorporating as much humus (well-rotted vegetable matter) as possible.

Lastly, if you haven't yet bought your first garden, don't even go and view houses unless they've got a sunny, south-facing aspect at the rear of the house. With a new house, check out the back garden and see what is or isn't growing. Pick up a handful of soil and sniff it – does it smell sweet?

Why did it die?

I think that some plants, such as the irresistible large-flowered clematis, should arrive with a label announcing their life expectancy. If it said something like 'two years if you're lucky', there'd be less disappointment around. I found a list of clematis I'd planted, thirty-two of them, sometime in the early 1980s. There's a scruffy note on the side, dated 1985, announcing: 'If no tick, means it's disappeared.' Even then, 'Daniel Deronda', 'Countess of Lovelace' and 'Mrs Cholmondeley' had no tick. Now, all thirty-two of them have gone except one, the inestimable 'Perle d'Azur'. The usual cause is clematis wilt, a disease which often happens just when the plant's looking really promising and covered in buds. Some or all of the plant collapses and then dies. Always distressing.

The most embarrassing cause of death in the garden is strangulation. The worst case is when you get one of those thick rubber tree ties and position it neatly around the trunk of a newly planted tree, fasten the buckle firmly to a stake and forget all about it. Fast-growing sappy plants such as fuchsias can be on their last gasp after only weeks of being tied to a cane with those innocuous-looking green plastic-covered ties. Climbers tied to wires stretched horizontally on walls are particularly easy to overlook.

If a coroner had to specify cause of death in this garden, the most common would be getting squashed. In the great competition for survival, in the never-ending desire for light, space, food and moisture, you can divide plants into those that do the squashing and those that get squashed – the squashees. International power struggles have got nothing on life in the garden. When two different species are planted side by side, one will invariably dominate. It doesn't matter how often I adjust the planting: the balance always shifts. One warm, rainy week in summer and small plants become overshadowed by the local bullyboys, such as opium poppy seedlings – only 3cm/1in high when last seen. Seven days later, and they've become an impenetrable, light-excluding thicket. Or one of the big running thugs, such as the willowherb (*Chamerion angustifolium*, 1.2m/4ft), in one of its beautiful forms such as 'Stahl Rose' or 'Album'.

'Killed by love' is another inscription found in the garden graveyard. For any hope of recovery, potted plants that have had one splash too many, sullen looking with droopy leaves and a heavy wet pot, go into the potting shed (so I'm nowhere near them when I have the watering can in hand). Overfeeding might not actually kill but causes plants to grow too gross and flowerless – the lie-on-the-sofa-with-a-packet-of-crisps effect. Plants such as the perennial wallflowers *Erysimum* 'Bowles' Mauve', *E.* 'Dawn Breaker' and *E. cheiri* 'Harpur Crewe' and the perennial stock (listed under *Matthiola* perennial stock) are examples of the many plants best underfed.

Rose 'William Lobb' is strong enough to compete with *Chamerion angustifolium* 'Stahl Rose'.

'Divided at the wrong time of year' could be the epitaph for some plants, such as grasses, *Aster amellus* (60cm/24in) cultivars, and somewhat tender plants such as kniphofia and agapanthus. Never divide these in autumn, when the soil is too cold for them to re-establish. Wait until spring.

If a plant is going to die, I wish it would do so fast, and not sulk for years. A dead twig here, a yellowing shoot there, and what about the odd pink pustules on the dead wood at the back? Could be coral spot fungus. The genus *Daphne* are particularly prone to fading away. Whereas *D. tangutica* Retusa Group and *D. bholua* are survivors, the daphnes that used to be here, from *D. arbuscula* and *D. petraea* to *D. genkwa*, with melted amethyst flowers, are all divinely scented and all dead. However, I discovered recently that even when dying an oak tree, which can take hundreds of years to actually fall down, is home to a vast array of small wildlife.

Then there's death by treading on snouts in spring and death by cutting back too hard (you were annoyed it grew larger than expected). 'It died on me,' you hear people say in Ireland – as E.A. Bowles (a great early twentieth-century garden writer and plantsman) remarked, 'that mild reproach and suggestion of wilful suicide . . . which so neatly lays the blame on the plant'. The reality is you killed it. Perhaps the universal cause of most garden deaths is that the garden owner, you or I, forgot all about the plant in the first place . . .

The one-hour-a-week garden

Gardens seem to get smaller at precisely the same rate as mortgages get bigger. Tiny gardens and whopping mortgages. Combine the two. Add a young family. Knackered at weekends, exhausted in the evening, in order to cope you must scrumple up your life and squeeze it into a ball like a piece of newspaper. There's no time left for gardening. Besides, the few minutes you have should be spent as recovery time, standing in your garden and learning to breathe, instead of doing the eyes-down, hard slog of yesterday's gardener. The other day I started to think about how to make a garden requiring less than an hour's work a week.

Be generous with space you allow for a paved or decked living area. Allow yourself a few very large containers. Organize a tap to be installed very near the containers.

In our garden there are two large gravelled areas: one developed around 2003 in the area that used to be an oval lawn, the other in the front garden. They demand practically no work. Admittedly (this is essential) the soil was clean of perennial weeds at the start. We forked the area over and levelled it with a rake. Then we firmed it – by walking backwards and forwards with little shuffling steps, feet kept close together. We removed any large stones and raked it again. We planted large plants or trees, before spreading about 10–15cm/4–6in of washed pea gravel over the area. Gravel with small stones is nice and quiet to walk on. Larger stones, despite being better burglar alarms, make for uncomfortable walking, like a beach where the pebbles are too big. Remember, though, that gravel doesn't work on a slope: you have to level it and build low retaining walls to form a series of terraces.

I'm repeatedly asked why I don't use the horticultural fabric sold as weed suppressant under the gravel. Apart from the fact that I can't bear to see a bit of the fabric sticking out, I love the freedom of not having it. I haven't seen a sniff of a weed, in either area, since the gravel went on. Planting is quick: you just scrape the gravel to one side and plant the plant in the usual way, firm round the soil and tuck the gravel back under the plant's leaves. Plants enjoy the coolness beneath the gravel, a condition that often mimics how they

Aralia elata, the bamboo *Phyllostachys vivax* f. *aureocaulis*, *Hedychium forrestii* (hardy here if mulched in winter) and English marigolds in the gravel garden

would grow in the wild. However, I admit that gravel needs topping up more often without the fabric. I've also noticed that dog mess takes longer to disappear when this material is in place.

Only growing small plants because you have a small space isn't a valid rule. There's a little garden near here that's the proud possessor of an enormous *Gunnera manicata* (1.8m/6ft) growing in the corner. I suspect its roots are somewhere in the main drain. The remainder of the garden has been taken over by grass and flowering weeds forming a gentle contrast to the whopping gunnera leaves. It looks amazing.

So, buy some great big grasses – the giant reed (*Arundo donax*, 3m/10ft, a nuisance in hot climates), *Miscanthus sinensis* 'Cosmopolitan' (1.8m/6ft) or *M. sacchariflorus* (1.5m/5ft), or a big bamboo. Bamboos are cliché plants but terrific value for presence and screening. If you can manage to place a small tree so that it doesn't shade your patch, so much the better.

I adore *Melianthus major* (2.5m/8ft) for its super-sized, sculpted, pale blue big leaves. I'd plant pink and white Japanese anemones (*Anemone* x *hybrida*, 1.5m/5ft) in the shade and loads of rosemary (excellent tolerator of neglect) in the sun. Get a good blue form of *Rosmarinus officinalis* (90cm/3ft) such as 'McConnell's Blue' or 'Sissinghurst Blue'. Lovely blue forms grow here, but I've still got a wishy-washy form that I brought with me from London years ago, as I don't want to remove it because of the superstition 'Where the rosemary thrives the woman is strong.' Lavenders, perovskias, yuccas, erodiums, euphorbias, catmints, thymes and origanums are all lovely easy plants for sun. Shrubs I'd include would be the Mexican orange (*Choisya ternata*, 2m/7ft) and any form of *Rosa rugosa* (1.2m/4ft), the toughest of roses.

I'd add *Fuchsia magellanica* var. *molinae* (2m/7ft) to the anemones in the shade, but then I like it so much that I'd add this South American shrub to every garden. *F. magellanica* itself, naturalized in many places including Ireland, has crimson and purple flowers like earrings, but *F.m.* var. *molinae* has white flowers washed in palest pink with pale lilac underskirts, which show up prettily against the green leaves. A mass of blossom for much of the year, it'll grow in sun or shade, and it doesn't mind a bit whether you prune it a lot, a little or not at all.

But, I hear you thinking, what about the work? You will have to rake the gravel occasionally. Some plants will need cutting back once a year – the grasses, anemones, catmints and perovskias, for example. You might have to wave the secateurs at the lavenders and thymes. But even if you do nothing, your place outside will be wonderful, a place to sniff the air and watch the bumblebees go by.

Kniphofia 'Erecta', a rare poker, has florets that turn upwards as they mature. It is seen here with tall miscanthus and banana in the gravel garden.

Acer griseum is fairly slow, so it's worth buying a decent specimen to begin with.

Ten trees for a small garden

The less room you have, the more particular you must be about choosing a tree, and the more fussy about which ones are suitable. I've put in too many trees over the years and then had to take them out again. Those that tolerate pruning (a great help when you're adjusting space) are indicated below.

The paperbark maple (*Acer griseum*, height to 12m/40ft) is a beautiful small Chinese tree with shining cinnabar-red peeling bark, magical when slivers of bark are backlit by the sun. I've limbed up mine (taken off the lower branches), better to display the trunk and to allow light to the base of the tree for plants underneath. It's not a tree that casts too much shade (an important point for small gardens) and the leaves flare scarlet for one gorgeous week in autumn. I've learnt my lesson about the wonderful Japanese maples (*Acer palmatum* cultivars), which dislike dry, limey gardens and cold east spring winds. They're not for me. *A. griseum* is more tolerant.

I don't care if you see birches on every roundabout in Ireland. Birches give a lovely airy effect, the fluttering leaves casting a veil rather than a shadow. Here we grow *Betula utilis* 'Fascination' (20m/65ft), with its pinkish brown bark, bred by Jan Ravensburg here in Ireland, and 'White Light', bred by Buckley of County Limerick. But there are many other good birches. We've a good multi-stemmed specimen of *B. utilis* var. *jacquemontii* (20m/65ft); the leaves are a bit sparse, but the white bark is exquisite. I'm told the sap begins to rise very early with birches, so if you want to remove any lower limbs, do so soon after leaf fall in early winter (although recent Forestry Commission research recommends summer pruning for many trees). Established birches suck up moisture all around, so put your bulbs and ground cover in before the trees get big. A birch to beware of (I fell straight into the trap) is the one invariably recommended for small gardens, *Betula pendula* 'Youngii' (3.5m/11–12ft). Usually grafted, this matures into a blobby-looking bird's nest on a stick.

Luma apiculata, also known as *Myrtus apiculata* (10m/33ft), is listed in *The New Royal Horticultural Society Dictionary of Gardening* as zone 9, but I'm sure this very distinctive, slow-growing small tree is worth a try in zone 8. The beautiful, orange-brown, suede-like bark peels away to expose the creamy inner surface. Loved by bees, the white flowers in late summer make a good contrast to the dark evergreen leaves. Slow growing and deserving of a warm spot (ours is

Betula utilis 'Fascination' in the front garden, in November

growing on a south-facing wall), this Chilean tree looks even better if you plant a whole grove, as seen to wonderful effect in the mild climate of Mount Stewart, one of the world's great gardens in County Down, Northern Ireland, now owned by the National Trust. *Luma apiculata* doesn't mind being pruned.

The coyote willow (*Salix exigua*, 9m/30ft), from western North America and Mexico, is an elegant little willow, with silky, slender leaves that become more silvery and light catching as summer advances. An excellent choice for tiny gardens, as it can be stooled (cut down to about 90cm/3ft) every year. It looks good like this in a flowerbed. I have three and I should like more; as it runs at the root, they'll probably turn up.

The willow family are members of the great and the good, with one exception. Here again I fell headlong into the trap: *Salix caprea* 'Kilmarnock' (3m/10ft) is ostensibly a small weeping treasure, at least in spring, at the pussy willow stage. Usually, it's a very obviously grafted plant, often with great splodges of grafting wax visible. By late summer you'll notice that it's a plant worth avoiding: another blob on a stick with depressing leaves in dull green.

Every time I see *Prunus serrula* (height to 15m/50ft), one of the cherries, I wonder why I'm not growing it, for its marvellous, shining mahogany bark. Furthermore, the narrow, toothed leaves are not as gloomy looking as other cherries are in summer.

For years we grew *Cornus controversa* 'Variegata' (4m/12ft), which makes a wonderful specimen dogwood, best grown in an isolated position to show off the distinctive tiered habit and cream and green leaves. I used to think, however, even before it died of a fungus disease, that the variegated form of the pagoda dogwood (*C. alternifolia* 'Argentea', 3m/10ft) made a better garden plant – it invariably appeared healthier.

You have to respect a plant that has been in existence for 200 million years, as has the maidenhair tree (*Ginkgo biloba*, height to 30m/100ft). I saw it growing wild in China, where it is a very variable species. It is, in fact, a deciduous conifer, although the lobed leaves look exactly like those of an adiantum or maidenhair fern. They go a beautiful clear yellow before falling in late autumn (they colour much better in the USA than here). I love this tree, and wish we had space for it. You can find tall, slender, fastigiate (or sticking-up) cultivars. Tolerant of many conditions, gingko is not suitable for small gardens, but one can always dream, and we can at least see one over the wall in next-door's garden.

Crataegus orientalis (formerly *C. laciniata*, 7m/23ft) is a thorn tree with downy, silver-grey leaves. The fruits, which appear in quantity every second year or so, are like little orange-red apples. This also accepts pruning, and makes a good specimen tree.

The Siberian pea tree (*Caragana arborescens* 'Lorbergii', height to 6m/20ft) is really a shrub, but you can train it to look like a graceful, slow-growing little tree by limbing it up. Pale yellow pea flowers appear in May, set off by very fine linear leaves. The bark is like some strange, gilded, silky metal. 'Why not just leave it as a shrub?' you ask. Because in some garden situations a tree-like shape looks really good and shows off nearby planting. Be very sure you get the good cultivar 'Lorbergii', which casts very little shade, and that it's on its own roots (there are some inviting grafted plants around that mature into distorted specimens).

If we lived on lime-free soil, I'd grow one of the beautiful stewartia; and if I lived where the summers were hot, I'd grow the crepe myrtle (*Lagerstroemia indica*, 6m/20ft) – every time I see this wonderful small tree I long to grow it.

Quick-growing plants for young gardens

I must tell you about an inner-city garden. Small, empty of plants, surrounded by high brick walls, it's overlooked on two sides by a factory and an apartment block. Fortunately the sun streams in on the third side and, apart from a pile of rubble in one corner, the soil looks reasonably good. Three long granite steps, extending the full width of the site, lead up from the house. In the middle of the garden is a crisp, rectangular paved area, made of bricks, ideal for parties and sitting in the sun. A lovely simple design.

It's now early June, and the two owners, exhilarated by the thrill of actually having a garden, are itching to get started. Caution goes out of the door and enthusiasm takes over, so strong is the desire to see something green and growing. What we need are plants of the Jack-in-a-beanstalk category, plants that mean business, with rapid growth and oodles of presence.

Paulownia tomentosa (height to 20m/65ft) springs to mind. This Chinese tree has white to violet flowers and in sunnier climates it blooms when young. I first saw this beautiful foxglove tree in Battersea Park, London, and I couldn't understand why nobody had told me about it before. Naturalized in many parts of the world, it has become a roadside weed in the eastern United States. Nevertheless, weed or no weed, I'm mad about it. I love its enormous, downy leaves, up to 90cm/3ft across. I love the way you can almost see it grow. None of your namby-pamby stuff with paulownia. In future years, to obtain huge leaves, you stool it in spring, provide rich feeding and allow only one shoot to develop. It's best to let the plant settle for a year or so before doing this.

Another tree of amazingly rapid growth is the tree of heaven (*Ailanthus altissima*, 30m/100ft). The origin of the word *Ailanthus* is *ailanto,* a native name meaning 'reaching for the sky'. Particularly in the USA, hotter summers cause it to be a serious nuisance weed. It incontinently self-sows and overruns native vegetation. But in these temperate islands we admire the handsome, compound leaves with many leaflets, and the shining red new growths. For even larger leaves, treat the same way as the paulownia (see above). Lots of both will give a terrific instant effect.

I'm not quite sure what I think about eucalypts. Often I think they look alien when juxtaposed with our native trees such as oak, beech or hawthorn, but in a situation such as this enclosed city garden, a eucalyptus could be just what we want. Also, they often have superb juvenile leaves, in varying shades of duck-egg blue. In the mild coastal climate of the Mount Stewart garden, of particular note is the exquisite *Eucalyptus cinerea* (16m/52ft). If you're looking for a hardier, smaller eucalyptus for long-term planting, try *E. pauciflora* subsp. *niphophila* (6m/20ft). You can cut back eucalyptus annually in spring, so that they remain shrubby and never become trees, thus continuing to produce juvenile leaves.

'One of the most magnificent of all herbaceous plants,' remarked Graham Stuart Thomas of the cardoon (*Cynara cardunculus*, 1.5m/5ft). The leaves, 90cm/3ft or more in length, are luminous, silvery white and fern-like, their tips elegantly curving down towards the earth. Closely related to the globe artichoke, it has stout stems that are considered a delicacy when blanched, peeled, cooked and eaten, but few people here grow it for the table. Cardoons make a great addition to any planting with their sensational mounds of foliage. They love sun, warmth and good drainage.

Back to our city garden. It's not too late to put in some dahlias, and it would be a nice opportunity to try out the tree dahlia, the 3m/10ft high (here in Ireland, much taller in the wild) *D. imperialis*. The Aztecs used the hollow stems in its native South America to pipe domestic water from mountain springs. In our garden the imperial dahlia lives outside in a protected corner of the terrace, but I've yet to see it flower. Apparently the flowers are soft mauve.

As it's still early June, there's plenty of time to put in some big tropical-looking stuff such as bananas. Wigwams of runner beans and climbing French beans will add instant height. Grapevines will be planted on the sunniest wall, with courgette plants rambling beneath. Any remaining spaces will be filled with cosmos in mixed colours (we can't get trays of single-colour seedlings at this time of year), the big fragrant white tobacco plant *Nicotiana sylvestris* (1.5m/5ft), plus lots of nasturtium seeds sown now. By autumn there'll be a feast of colour, scent and good things to eat.

Cynara cardunculus, the cardoon, with crown imperials and narcissus, in April

The pros and cons of instant plants

Before the advent of the garden centre, a rewarding source of plants was the charity plant sale. You never knew what might turn up, although the more interesting items were often squirrelled away on arrival. Elders of the horticultural society running the sale would be seen poring over a box of donated plants at the entrance. You'd never quite catch what was said in these hurried discussions, but there'd be a sudden rustle of newspaper, a flash of green, and plants would vanish into boxes beneath the table (invariably covered in a cloth so that you couldn't see what was underneath).

Next to have their pick of the box would be those senior members who had generously offered their time to manage the 'Rare plants' stand. You'd see books being consulted and plants being studied critically as they were passed around at the back of the stall. You might even see a plant divided into two, for further distribution to the helpers then and there. A junior member would then be dispatched, with the now depleted box, to the more mundane sales tables marked 'Perennials' or 'Shrubs'.

At the end of the day the kindly people who ran these latter stands, who had neither the push nor the manoeuvring skills to position themselves better, were left to sell indeterminate bits of plant material wrapped in soggy paper, plus a motley collection of small plants in yoghurt pots.

I always believed that you began a garden with small plants, either from a sale or by post from a nursery (after much deliberation over the catalogue). Or, in the long slow days before garden centres, I'd be given plants after an invitation to a garden lunch, following which there'd be a leisurely circuit of the garden, accompanied by much debate about correct plant names. Then there'd be a proper sit-down tea in the dining room with thin sandwiches (crusts off, naturally), scones, homemade jam and Victoria sponge cake. At the end, the question I'd been waiting for: 'Is there any plant you want?'

I've always thought that whenever one gets to the stage of remarking 'Whatever is the world coming to?' it's the beginning of the end. Determined not to get into that frame of mind, I decided recently that I needed a more contemporary attitude. So, immediate satisfaction being just so 'now' (for the measured style that involves the slow nurture of seedling plants to maturity is disappearing), off I set for a wholesale nursery in County Kildare and ordered a 5m/16ft tall *Magnolia grandiflora* (height to 30m/100ft) in an enormous pot. Although it goes against everything in my yoghurt-pot-raised sensibility, being suddenly free to make an astonishing difference to a view by planting a large evergreen was terrific. I recommend it. Furthermore, I love the idea of buying time. When I realized that *Acer griseum* (12m/40ft – see page 53) was a tardy grower, I replaced it with a larger specimen, reckoning I'd thus saved five years' waiting time. And I well understand the joy of being able to plant a 2m/7ft yew or hornbeam hedge rather than waiting for years. However, it's said that by using the opposite method, and beginning your hedge with small, bare-rooted (not container-grown) plants, lifted from the open ground in winter, the resulting hedge will overtake the instant sort.

Magnolia grandiflora

A landscaper friend explained one of the reasons why mature trees in large containers fail when transplanted. The contents of the container require a large, deep hole to accommodate them. The hole goes down to impervious clay subsoil, where it acts as a sump; water collects; the tree's roots drown.

I suppose the ideal is a balance between the old-fashioned gift and the full-sized, in-flower plant from the garden centre. That is the case especially with roses – we've grown many from cuttings, taken from plants growing in old gardens where the owner has forgotten the name. 'Marie Pavic' is one such. We think a lot of this soft pink rose with a beautiful fragrance, blooming much of the year. And if I hadn't been to a garden lunch with Frances Hart, who's now ninety-four and lives just round the corner in Morehampton Road, we wouldn't be blessed with such a lovely, gentle-tempered easy rose.

Pests

I love drifting around the garden in a daze, just noticing lovely things. I don't want to think about infelicities of planting, or weeds, or any kind of ugliness, and I especially don't want to think about slugs. However, if Val and I set off on a tour together, we're hardly past the greenhouse (we always go round the garden anti-clockwise, sunny-side first) when his conversation turns to slugs. After that I can't stop visions sliding into my head that refuse to be rinsed away.

In the evening, throughout the year, we place plastic saucers (the ones used underneath pots) around the garden, filled with cheap lager (apparently slugs aren't particular). We put down between ten and fifty traps, depending on how warm and damp the weather is. Slugs are attracted, fall in and drown, but on subsequent nights, when the beer's no longer fresh, you won't catch any more. During our tour, numbers are mentioned: 'At least thirty caught last night,' (and that's just one saucer) Val will inform me, as if he was discussing the game bag after a shoot.

But I don't care how many were, or were not, destroyed. I read once that however many slugs you kill, the population will quickly readjust in relation to the food available, and there's a tasty diet always available here. Last summer I went to a talk entitled 'How to get Fond of a Snail'. Apparently these gastropods spend many hours twisting themselves round each other in a ballet of courtship. At least snails have a shell, dry to the touch, so I don't mind picking them up and throwing them into the bushes opposite, whereas I can't bear the slimy feel of a slug.

There are around 73,000 plants listed in the *RHS Plant Finder*, all available at the wave of a credit card. With such a choice I've decided life's too short to grow the gastropod gourmet plants; I'd sooner grow something else. But I still grow a few slug delicacies – *Senecio pulcher* (60cm/24in), for example, a frost-tender magenta perennial daisy from South America which resides on the raised bed, rarely seen without its attendant saucer of beer. (I've got a particular admiration for any plant in the senecio family, considering they are relations of the weed groundsel *Senecio vulgaris*, and I enjoy remarking to myself, as I walk by, 'Nice plant – pity about the relations.')

There's been much heartache here at Sandford Road on account of vine weevil. Some plants, such as *Heuchera*, are so heavily attacked by its grubs that I decided that rather than use chemicals

Slug bar

I would dig up the plants once a year, pick out the grubs and replant. The problem was that every time I walked past the heucheras, I'd picture what might be happening to the roots underground – almost certainly a horde of plump, creamy-white, segmented grubs stuffing their faces at my expense. Then I'd have to dig the plants up to check. Nearly always my suspicions were correct. My digging them up wasn't much good for them either, so finally I took out all the heucheras and used *Persicaria microcephala* 'Red Dragon' (60cm/24in) instead. This offers a beautiful fresh-looking mound of deep burgundy leaves patterned in silver all summer long, without any worries about what's happening underground. (I'm told it's invasive in warmer climates.)

I don't enjoy remembering that when I lived in London my favourite restaurant was L'Escargot in the West End, where I never failed to order snails with garlic butter. The only good thing I can think of to say about these garden molluscs is that occasionally the slime has a pretty mother-of-pearl look, iridescent, like the nail varnish that came from Woolworth's in the 1960s.

Plants for sunny walls

You'd think that the south-facing wall of the house would be the easiest place to choose plants for. After all, it's just the spot for trying out plants too tender for your existing climate. Quite. But I've changed plants more often here, and done more experimenting (a polite way of saying that I dug the plant up and replaced it with something I fancied more), than anywhere else in the garden. For me, the problem with a sunny south wall is that it's such a favoured position I can't decide which plants have truly earned enough stars to occupy it.

One of my first victims was *Rosa banksiae* 'Lutea' (6m/20ft). I read all about it. It sounded divine. Indeed it is, with lots of shiny green leaves and cascades of pale yellow double flowers in May. But nobody told me that this is a very wide plant, about 3m/10ft, which means that the rose bulged its way over much of the terrace and we could barely get by. Fine, I thought: I'll just prune it neatly back to the wall. But that doesn't work, because this rose flowers only on old wood. So, it was either tidy rose/no flowers or flowers/blockage on terrace. The rose went. In came *Luma apiculata* (10m/33ft) in its place.

I had a lot of bother with *Clematis armandii* (6m/20ft), a spectacular evergreen climber with glossy leaves and trusses of scented white waxy flowers in spring. If this is cleverly planted, it looks glorious. In my case it leapt straight up the wall, leaving a lot of leafless, gnarled, unattractive wood at the base, the nearest thing to varicose veins of the horticultural kind. If I'd planted it so that the base was unnoticed in the shade, we'd have seen the flowers nicely framed in foliage without the dirty underclothes. I tried pruning it hard back and training the new growth horizontally, which was a success for a time – at least until I wanted to try something else.

We inherited a wisteria, not a very good form, with rather stubby flowers. Although this one eventually died, a good wisteria would be one of my first choices for a southern aspect. To me there's no scent that better suggests sun and early summer warmth. Be careful to buy a cultivar with long, elegant racemes of flowers, for you don't want to wait years for a seed-grown plant to present you with washy mauve

Salvia microphylla var. *microphylla* has been thriving beside a sunny wall for thirty years. All the same, I take cuttings of this, as of most salvias, for extra security.

chubby flowers. Only the best will do. A good option is to buy your plant in bloom at a garden centre.

It's essential to prune your wisteria correctly; otherwise all you'll have will be a mad tangle of growth and a few flowers hidden by greenery. A simplified version of pruning to encourage formation of flower buds is to cut all growths back several times after midsummer during the growing season to five or six buds, except a few (say three to start with) of the longest growths for tying in to form the framework. Check over the pruned growths in winter and prune them again to two or three buds.

Although you'd barely notice the flowers of *Vitis vinifera* 'Incana' (15m/50ft, unpruned), and the blackbirds eat any fruit in autumn, I adore the leaves of this decorative grape, for their silky, silver-green downy leaves, in the age-old shape of a vine leaf. I have to remember to prune it in midwinter before the sap rises. In late summer it's prone to mildew, but that doesn't matter much, as the leaves already look as if they were dusted in powder.

You might wonder how I could possibly bring myself to take out an established *Bomarea caldasii* (4–5m/14–16ft), the beautiful South American climber related to alstroemeria. Granted, two or three umbels of glowing orange tubular blooms with flecked interiors did indeed turn up, to our great delight, most, but not all, autumns. However, two or three umbels were not enough, considering we had to put up with a whole season's tattered-looking leaves because it only flowers on growth made the previous year. Lovely plant. It didn't survive the move.

Decaisnea fargesii (3–5m/10–16ft) met the same fate (although it survived being transplanted to a less superior position). An easily grown Chinese shrub, this is pretty in spring, as the growing tips are flushed with navy blue. The flowers, which open early, are not blatantly showy but nice in a greeny yellow, quiet, well-bred sort of way. The pods of the fruit are startling, like fat, navy blue, slightly warty broad beans. Inside the pods are black beans, protected by smelly, sticky-looking gel. Decaisnea enjoys decent soil and is easily propagated from its beans. The problem on the terrace was that by late summer the leaves were yellowing and autumnal, and the fresh, it's-still-summer effect was spoilt everywhere else on the terrace. So we've moved it up to the far end of the garden, and in its former position there's a New Zealand lobster claw (*Clianthus puniceus*, 5m/16ft). The flowers are exactly as the common name suggests, the pale red of a just-boiled lobster. I've had this showy member of the pea family before – I don't find it very long lived. Flowered wood should be pruned out after flowering and young shoots trained in to horizontal wires on the wall.

The longest-surviving members of the plant congregation on the terrace are two abutilons, *A. megapotamicum* (2.5m/8ft) and a pretty yellow large-flowered cultivar without a name, which came from my home in Scotland. I used to grow the former in its popular variegated form. I then decided that the mottled yellow leaves overwhelmed the sweet little dangling red and yellow flowers, and Nature's original choice of dull green for the leaves was a far more fitting background.

Brazilian *A. megapotamicum* is a lovely easy-going plant, blooming for months on end, and worth growing in a pot if you live in a cold climate.

To really benefit plants grown near walls the first thing you should do is stretch good-quality wire horizontally, at roughly 60cm/24in intervals apart, running the wire through vine eyes (pieces of metal, about 10cm/4in long, with one end sharp to go into the wall and a ring at the other end to support the wire). This means that when you tie the stem of the plant to the wire, the stem is supported a few centimetres out from the wall, where there's plenty of air. Otherwise, the plant will be jammed up too close and greenfly and other pests will be more troublesome. (Note: You wouldn't want to be in hearing distance when I'm trying to get vine eyes to (a) go into the mortar of old walls and (b) stay there.)

Abutilon megapotamicum can be lightly pruned in spring.

Evergreen plants for walls

No sooner does a blank wall present itself than we're compelled to plant something – growing up it, rambling over it or forming a great bulging shrub to conceal it. An empty stretch of wall will not be tolerated, especially when it's built of cement blocks, which it often is. (I'd disguise this straight away with some well-made trellis rather than being in a rush to plant.)

The evergreen *Trachelospermum jasminoides* (7m/23ft) is an especially nice climber, though not a plant for cold gardens. It has shining deep green leaves, thick to the feel, and deliciously scented small cream flowers around August. We've grown the variegated form, *T.j.* 'Variegatum', on a south wall for over thirty years and it's never been bothered by cold. The foliage is a pretty mix of pale green and cream, washed pink in winter. Furthermore, here it lives on the smell of an oily rag – poor soil, not much space for its roots and no watering. *T. asiaticum*, with more slender leaves, is considered hardier. The leaves of both flush purple in cold weather. Prune or don't – whatever you like. Both need tying in to their supports when young.

There are few self-clinging climbers and one of the most useful is ivy (*Hedera* spp.). The thing to remember about ivy is that *you* must remain in charge: look the other way for a moment and it will have got away. Ivy is a curious plant: there can be two different forms – the climbing, and the flowering and fruiting form. First, in what is known as the juvenile stage, the ivy whizzes up, clinging as it goes, as fast as you allow it, to the top of its support – wall, tree, house or whatever; then, as soon as it reaches the top, the habit of the plant changes. This is the arborescent or tree-like stage. Now the ivy stops clinging and turns woodier, and the leaves alter considerably, becoming less shapely and more entire. Flowers arrive in early autumn (attractive to many insects including wasps, moths and honeybees), followed by fruit (attractive to blackbirds). Thirty-five years ago I planted variegated *Hedera colchica* 'Sulphur Heart' (climber) to clothe a high trellis, but I wish I'd put in plain green to form a neutral background. We've managed to stay on top for all that time – just. You have to be careful when ivies reach their arborescent form: they become so heavy that they can pull down their supports in a gale.

Itea ilicifolia (seen here with spotted aucuba) has heavenly night-time scent.

From the gardener's point of view, walls and climbers are eternally bracketed together. Thinking of covering a wall? We go immediately to the section marked 'Climbers' in the garden centre. But what about the many non-climbing shrubs that form lovely bulging buttresses, while enjoying the extra comforts of wall protection?

Not all shrubs look appropriate when planted as a backdrop to a flower border, but *Bupleurum fruticosum* (3m/10ft) acts as a back-of-stage curtain for all the colours in front. Smooth evergreen leaves with a bluish cast look smart year round. My plant has allowed its branches to wander up through a nearby pittosporum, so the acid yellow, long-lasting, late-summer flowers, shaped like cow parsley or Queen Anne's lace, wave from a height of 6m/20ft. Tolerant of dry soil, this seeds itself lightly, but I haven't found it easy to grow from cuttings; trimming or even hard pruning is acceptable when required.

Apparently, in its native California, *Carpenteria californica* (2m/7ft) has a very restricted range. When it's looking its best, this is a beautiful shrub, with evergreen leaves and flowers in pristine white with gold stamens, certainly warranting space on your sunniest wall. But the leaves can look shabby at times, and it needs regular picking over to tidy it up – therefore plant it somewhere with easy access. For years I grew a poor form of carpenteria, with small flowers, and

Carpenteria californica

not many of them (it was probably seed raised), until eventually I replaced it with the good cultivar 'Ladhams' Variety'. (By the way, a small grumble as a gardening reader: why is 'pure' so often attached to 'white'? I suppose Persil has its tentacles everywhere.)

Before my time, Augustine Henry, the famous Irish plant collector (1857–1930), used to live next door at 47 Sandford Road. He discovered *Itea ilicifolia* (5m/16ft) growing near the Yangtze Gorge in China. My cutting, from the original plant in his garden, makes a large, lax shrub on our north-facing wall, with evergreen holly-like leaves and cool, pale green, very long (30cm/12in) elegant racemes of tiny flowers. In the evening, it's hard to decide exactly where the dreamy fragrance begins or ends. Here for a moment, gone the next, but it lingers overnight and wafts over the wall to the back door as I go out in the morning.

I could never love a pyracantha. These tough evergreen shrubs remind me of earnest, somewhat boring people. But I admit they have excellent green leaves and bright shiny berries, and they do look good neatly trained, cordon fashion, to a wall. The ubiquitous (here, at any rate) Mexican orange blossom (*Choisya ternata*, 2m/7ft), has deliciously aromatic foliage when crushed, and is a terrific evergreen for tolerating dryish shade.

Difficult places

Narrow alleys between houses are draughty places where the wheelie bin reigns supreme. There may be room for only the bin – with or without one of those flowery plastic would-be disguises – plus a few containers. You'd probably be better paving or tiling the whole area and installing plenty of lighting. Perhaps a compost bin would fit in here? The leafmould store? The wormery? Or it might be a handy place to store plants in pots (that you've got bored with), all ready to land on the next unsuspecting person. Anything that can be kept here will release more growing space elsewhere. Give this some thought.

Near houses, surrounded by buildings, I'd be longing for the colour green. Yesterday I was sitting in the hairdresser's down the road. Invisible as far as the young goddesses who worked there were concerned, as anyone over forty is, I had plenty of time to admire the tiny yard behind. Just a small rectangle with high walls. The whole of one side was the glass window of the hairdresser's, one whole wall was painted Madonna's dress blue and the other two were white. Three large containers were planted respectively with one large green bamboo, a plain green phormium and a *Fatsia japonica* (a handsome, large glossy-leaved evergreen shrub, very shade tolerant, 3m/10ft). Yesterday the ceiling was blue sky, so there were only three colours to see – blue, white and the green of plants. Very simple and effective.

Bamboos would cast a lovely veil of fluttering green, but in a container they'd be only a short-term solution, as their roots won't tolerate restriction for more than a year or two. And they'd need regular watering and a promise of freedom in the open garden pretty soon. The more plain green the better. Forget your glamorous fancy stuff – bright colours would look out of place here. What we're looking for are plants that flourish in adversity.

If you have a slightly wider space at the side of your house, the position may still be challenging, but you'll probably have room for planting beds. *Geranium macrorrhizum* (30cm/12in) will not only put up with poor living but looks pleased about it. The leaves are sticky and aromatic with a distinct, refreshing scent – the source of oil of geranium. The flowers are pale magenta in the species itself, but there's also white 'Album' and pale pink 'Ingwersen's Variety'. *G. macrorrhizum* is

Rubus tricolor confined to an Ali Baba pot

Variegated ground elder in a Canadian garden, kept under control by the lawnmower

often described as a ground-cover plant – I remember Mrs Knox Finlay (a great Scots plantswoman) remarking what an insult it was to refer to a plant thus. But you need a great big patch of this for it to look anything. *Geranium procurrens* (30cm/12in) from the Himalayas is another stalwart survivor with purple-pink flowers and black veins. This whizzes along in dry shade, forming roots at each leaf node as it goes.

Rubus tricolor (sprawler), a relation of the blackberry, is a prostrate, evergreen shrub. You see it used on the side of motorways, on steep banks and on roundabouts. But it looks remarkably good planted in a tall container (such as an Ali Baba pot, or something more contemporary) in an uninspiring corner, with long trails of dark green, bristly, light-reflecting leaves. Planted in the open ground it would be over into next-door's garden in a flash, but when its boundless exuberance is under control, it forms a well-behaved option for long life in a container.

Ground elder, one of the noxious gang of weeds, has a very pretty variegated but equally territorial form in *Aegopodium podagraria* 'Variegatum' (45cm/18in). To start with it'll sit there all nicey-nicey, when all the while it's taking over underground. Graham Stuart Thomas remarked: 'The person who gave you that plant is not a friend.' That made me think. In a Canadian garden I saw the variegated ground elder brilliantly used: it was planted in a wide ribbon between the edge of a lawn and natural woodland. Whenever the elder ventured a shoot into the grass, the mower chopped it off. Nobody cared what it did in the wood.

Vanishing tools

There are two distinct types of gardener. One goes outside and makes an amazing mess. Within minutes, weeds, tools, deadheads and buckets are scattered everywhere. This is the type who treats the flowerbed like a trampoline, trots down the path with muddy boots for a telephone call, doesn't bother to take the boots off at the back door, and finally sits down in the kitchen and demands a cup of tea. This mode of gardening is fine. I did just that. Then, when I realized how much good gardening time was wasted in cleaning up afterwards, I became the other sort of gardener. I tidy up as I go. How smug.

I don't know what happens here, but I swear that tools have minds of their own. There must be at least seven brooms. We never stop sweeping, as we've lots of paths and paving, and plenty of blackbirds, who love rootling about, scattering soil as they go. Ideally, I like one broom for the greenhouse, another for the potting shed and a third for the alpine house (the small greenhouse that is stopped from falling down by layer upon layer of gloss paint). You wouldn't believe that all three could disappear overnight, but they do. There must be witches around, despite an elder (*Sambucus nigra*, 6m/20ft) growing near the garden door (this is supposed to keep them away). There's another brush that's meant to be kept by the trellis halfway up the garden, to reduce trips back to the yard to fetch one. I keep meaning to tie it to the trellis with a padlock, so often does it vanish.

However, my personal record of lost secateurs is worse. If they didn't have red handles (invariably they're made by the excellent Felco), I reckon I could lose two pairs a day. I imagine them somersaulting into the buckets of rubbish, secreting themselves in the middle and hoping to escape via the compost heap. Even if I leave them parked on top of box topiary, so that I couldn't possibly miss the red handles against the green box, when I return to fetch them they've usually scarpered.

Trowels can be worse. I like stainless-steel ones the best, but these are the first to go missing. Then I'm left with the ones to be avoided, which usually have jolly bright-coloured handles set at a peculiar angle to the digging bit of the trowel. The peculiar angle makes your hand ache to

The garden entrance from the yard, with our tools hanging on the wall

put any weight on them, and if you do manage to push them into the soil they go into terminal bend, from which they never recover. But you can't actually bring yourself to throw them away, so they hide at the back of the shed under some sacks until one day, when you've lost every other trowel in the place, you find a whole heap of them. But by then, you've forgotten that they're the bendy ones. Exasperation.

There's one great pet among the many tools here: a tiny fork on the end of a long handle. We've had it for thirty-six years. The metal part is shiny and half worn away with use, and the wooden handle has the wonderful feel of a good antique piece of furniture that I can only describe as 'lovingly polished by housemaids for the last one hundred years'. It means that you can stand on the path and tweak out a weed without treading on the bed; you can spear leaves from a distance on a wet winter's day; you can ruffle up the soil when there's a footmark.

Having broken many spades with wooden handles, we now have a stainless-steel spade that's well made and light. Be careful of the cheaper ones – they can be too heavy. Having lived here in Ireland for thirty-six years, after starting life in Scotland, I'm still in the dark about some local expressions, for example 'digging with the left foot'. I know it's a way of informing whoever you're talking to about what religion somebody is, that is Catholic or Protestant. The problem is, I've yet to find out which way round it is. Some people mean one thing, some the opposite. By the way, I myself dig with the right foot.

Collapse of late-summer garden

You can't take away the beauty of early summer. Whatever you do, beech trees still unfurl their tender green, the ditches are frothing cow parsley and the sun has real warmth at last. Even a neglected garden looks heavenly when all the different shades of green are so distinct.

There's about one week in early June when all is serene and I feel totally up to date with garden work. Deadheading and watering are only just starting, the summer bedding is settling in and the first flush of weeds have been dealt with. You need to enjoy this brief respite.

Late summer is another matter. Hot drying winds and thirsty plants, and the diversity of leaf colours mellow to a uniform, dusty green. This is the point when gardeners lose heart, complain that their gardens are disintegrating and go abroad in disgust.

There are three fundamental ways of rescuing your late-summer garden: one is to spruce up and look after what's there already; the second is to use lots of plants that have a long flowering season; and the third is to use plenty of plants that truly belong to late summer and early autumn.

To begin with the sprucing up: the further summer progresses, the more fidgeting, tweaking, tidying, brushing, staking, re-staking, pinching out, watering, liquid feeding, weeding, deadheading and pruning of over-energetic plants occupy my time. I spend many hours circling the garden; then I go round immediately after and find as much to do as I did the first time. It's a sort of repetitive compulsive disorder – I can't stop. I may have to give it up, just as I've had to deal with drink, cigarettes, rich food and all things nice and addictive.

How is it that when you get a real stunner of a good plant, which provides months of flowers and masses of colour – dahlias, petunias or begonias, say, or a Hybrid Tea rose for that matter – the elders of the gardening world then decide that these plants are just too bourgeois? The antonym of these is epitomized by some obscure plant, with a very small, preferably green flower, that's difficult to grow, such as *Bupleurum angulosum* (40cm/16in) – of which I'm particularly fond. Even *The New Royal Horticultural Society Dictionary of Gardening* begins its description with 'stem leafy with numerous dead leaves at base'. How inviting. (Seriously, the colour is rather delicious, a sort of jade green, but I've tried it several times and it keeps on dying.)

What worries me is that alstroemerias, most commendable plants for many reasons, not least that they bloom for months, are likely to go the way of all good plants, and become so common that nobody will be seen dead with them. I already suspect that they have appeared once too often in vases on the tables of hotel dining rooms.

Orange Chilean *Alstroemeria aurea* (90cm/3ft), in cultivation since the 1830s, always suffered from its reputation for running at the roots, and later the *A. ligtu* hybrids (90cm/3ft) became more popular for having pink, coral and salmon in the mix rather than the less popular orange. Some of the newer hybrids were originally bred as cut flowers, and eventually became available in the horticultural trade. These are beautiful plants, in many glorious shades, with clusters of large lily-like flowers with lovely speckled interiors. They love sun, good drainage and no root disturbance. When I obtain a new alstroemeria cultivar, I usually pot it on to a larger pot and build it up into a vigorous plant in the greenhouse before planting it out. These new hybrids flower here from May until early July, when they stop for a rest and begin again a few weeks later. I find that the dwarf cultivars available are not a bit nice and very squat.

The old-fashioned ligtu hybrids included some delicious shocking pinks. A good gardening friend, Warrene Hume, who with the optimism of a true gardener was still sowing lily seeds in her late eighties, told me how to propagate these: sow ripe seed and plant out the whole potful without separating the seedlings. Never disturb.

Now for the true late-season plants. When, in 1989, I first visited the USA, I was amazed to see, out of the window of the car meeting us at the airport, one of my favourite perennials growing in a ditch. Joe pye weed (*Eupatorium purpureum* subsp. *maculatum*, 2m/7ft), is a terrific plant, decorative from bud to bloom, with flat misty purple heads of lots of little flowers. The seedheads look good way into autumn. It needs a little staking and likes water by the canful in dry weather. The form we grow here has deep purple stems and exceptionally large flowers surrounded by extra small ones.

More late-summer/early-autumn plants: aconitum (several), actaea, amaryllis, anemone, aster, canna, ceratostigma, chrysanthemum, cosmos, crocosmia, dahlia, fuchsia, hemerocallis, kirengeshoma, kniphofia (some), *Lathyrus latifolius*, miscanthus, perovskia, phlox, salvia (many), sedum, tricyrtis.

Crocosmia x *masoniorum* 'Firebird' with seedheads of *Rodgersia pinnata* 'Perthshire Bronze' and silver leaves (top left) of *Desmodium yunnanense*

Tiger lilies with the dark lacy leaves of *Sambucus nigra* 'Eva'

Part 2

THE MIDDLE GROUND

Gravel gardens

Mountains have a compelling effect on me. I can't wait to struggle up them, wheezing as I go, to areas that appear barren and empty of anything green. Near the top, where the sun's hot and you don't feel it because the wind bites and the air's thin, you find exquisite small plants, huddling close to the ground, against the always untrustworthy weather. They are protected under a deep covering of snow for much of the year and their roots are anchored way down in the scree (deep beds of gravelly, rocky stones).

Negotiation of these steeply angled slopes is best described as being like skiing over stones rather than snow. Sometimes the whole precipitous bank of gravel (known as a mobile scree) starts to shift downhill. Scary indeed. But certain plants, such as the buttercup *Ranunculus semiverticillatus* (7cm/3in), in particular the blush-pink form, warrant any kind of frightening experience. This buttercup has flowers like water-lilies, floating on a sea of stones, and intricate, delicate grey-blue foliage; and you must tramp up to a great height in Chile and Argentina to view it. Once I see such plants at close quarters, and realize the extraordinary, stark conditions they inhabit, I know there's no chance whatsoever of them adapting to life in suburban Dublin. To see them takes away the craving to possess – such plants are not for captivity.

But whereas this jewel of a buttercup is not for transportation, the notion of placing a layer of gravel on the surface of the soil was stolen years ago by gardeners as a brilliant horticultural aid. This mulch is useful in five different ways: it protects the soil to some extent from frost; it helps control germination of weeds, such as annual meadow grass; slug travel arrangements are surely uncomfortable; it controls evaporation of moisture; and it unifies spotty planting. This last is particularly useful for plant addicts. Anything is good that stops a garden looking like a tasting menu for plants.

The raised bed, in full sun and well drained, with a gravelly mix and a gravel mulch, provides a safe home for plants that can't take a lot of competition. Salvias, yellow *Tropaeolum polyphyllum* and orange *Kniphofia thomsonii* var. *thomsonii* all thrive here.

Like the buttercup, *Tropaeolum polyphyllum* (prostrate) is a native of Chile and Argentina and under snow in winter, but it comes from a lower altitude. For the last thirty years, this

nasturtium relation has been growing here in the same sunny raised bed, where it drapes 90cm/3ft or more trails of glaucous (blue-green waxy coating like the bloom on grapes) foliage and bright yellow, nodding, helmet-like flowers. You see this plant either as a weakling, just about to die, or as a galloping invader. I was told that its rhizomes are capable of descending to 90cm/3ft below soil level (the reason it's impossible to divide, and therefore scarce). When some five years ago we changed the soil in this bed, excavating the old soil to almost 90cm/3ft deep, I was worried I'd lose *T. polyphyllum*, but not a bit of it: the following summer it was in better form than ever.

Many times, after failing with an elite small plant elsewhere in the garden, I've decided that I should find space for it on the raised bed. The advantages are many: plants are within easy reach for someone with a bad back; raised beds are by nature well drained, being higher than the natural soil level; they aren't so easily overshadowed, as the larger beds are; nearer eye level plants are easier to appreciate; and with luck the dogs will be too lazy to jump up to them.

There's nothing nicer than looking at plants and thinking how lovely they are. David Shackleton (himself a great plantsman) used to remark, 'The definition of a plantsman is someone who looks at every single one of his plants, every single day.' Then, of course, there's the Chinese saying that 'The best manure is the shadow of the gardener.'

Questionable plants

When we first arrived here I had the usual new owner's attitude of not daring to touch anything (quite right too: you need time to see what you've inherited for at least one season), but now, after thirty-six years, I'm looking at plants with a more critical eye.

For example, the *RHS Plant Finder 2005–2006* lists no fewer than 700 hardy geraniums available, of which there are 685 I can probably do without. I notice that there are over fifty available forms alone of *Geranium phaeum* (60cm/24in), the mourning widow geranium. There has to be some horticulturally correct way of describing small, mud-coloured flowers and leaves that sprawl about in a disordered state later in the season. I do agree that the white-flowered form, *G.p.* 'Album', is a refreshing sight in early summer. But you can keep the rest of this particular species. (Confusingly, when I hear the word 'geranium', I see a cheery picture of window boxes full of bright red flowers, but these tender plants are in fact pelargoniums.)

A plant that seems a swan when first acquired may turn out to be a goose, as happened here with the wire netting bush (*Corokia cotoneaster*, 2m/7ft). As a curiosity this is an interesting New Zealand shrub. They say that in order to prevent its leading shoot from being grazed by an extinct bird, the giant moa, this bulging shrub evolved into an extraordinary, complicated tangle of branches.

For years the wire netting bush grew in the middle of the border, acting as a misty, greyish background shrub. Or so I told myself. I didn't really notice as it slowly developed into what can only be described as a very large, thicket-like depressing blob, inhabited by a colony of sparrows. Last autumn we dug it up and the sparrows moved camp to a nearby pittosporum. Light and sunshine have flooded the space. A wonderful change. The important thing is to question the presence of everything, down to the last self-sown seedling. Each plant must merit its space.

Then there's the question of dying badly. One of the worst plants for being an absolute let-down is the variegated *Sisyrinchium striatum* 'Aunt May' (60cm/24in). There are two weeks in the year, around June, when this iris relation is full of appeal. The fans of leaves are smartly striped in grey-green and cream and refined spires of pale yellow flowers emerge. At this stage it is irresistible. For

Geranium 'Rozanne' blooms for months. 'Jolly Bee' is similar.

the remainder of the year the plant is clogged up with dirty leaves, some of them black, ruining the effect. Of course, it's nothing that half an hour with a sharp pair of scissors wouldn't fix . . .

I gave up long ago on late-summer blooming, carmine red *Clematis* 'Ville de Lyon' (climber, Z6). It probably hated me as much as I did it. We pruned it to 90cm/3ft each winter; things looked hopeful every spring; every summer it was a picture of unhappiness, with thin straggling brown stems, its few remaining leaves with crumpled edges and the inevitable powdering of mildew. Flowers, also mildewed, would be somewhere over the wall next door. Curiously, every time I search along a row of clematis at a garden centre, one of the first is invariably 'Ville de Lyon'.

The first time I saw *Acer pseudoplatanus* 'Brilliantissimum' (3m/10ft), a fancy form of sycamore, when its spring foliage was a gorgeous shrimp pink, I fell straight into the trap. Effectively, this is a ball on a stick, a lollipop tree, with none of the natural grace of a wild plant. Later in the season the spring pink bleaches to dry-looking yellowish green. But I suppose no amount of quiet nagging will prevent a novice gardener trying out such plants for themselves.

In contrast to the above, here are some hardy geraniums I really like: *Geranium* x *lindavicum* 'Lissadell' (15cm/6in), a lovely little silver-leaved plant with pink flowers in early summer; *G. sanguineum* var. *striatum* (15cm/6in), the pale pink form of the Irish native bloody cranesbill, only found on an island off Cumbria; *G. subcaulescens* (15cm/6in), a lovely neat mound of shocking magenta; *G.* 'Rozanne', 'Jolly Bee', 'Brookside' and 'Spinners'; and the heavenly, double violet *G. pratense* 'Plenum Violaceum' (90cm/3ft).

Plants worth searching for

Amicia zygomeris (1.5m/5ft), from woodland and riversides in Mexico, at around 2000m/6500ft, is an unusual plant that is herbaceous here in Ireland and disappears below ground level in winter, so although it is usually only hardy to zone 9 it could be worth trying in zone 7 with a deep mulch. The light green leaves close in the evening, giving a clue that it's a member of the pea family. Pleasant, chrome yellow flowers appear in September. But the remarkable feature of *Amicia* is its extraordinary, plump, bladder-like, purple-veined stipules at the leaf bases – they're so attractive you want to squeeze them. Sun loving and needing little attention, this is an easy plant; but, just in case, I take a few emergency cuttings in autumn.

Zone 9 is the considered growing zone for *Aloe striatula*, but this handsome South African succulent, from the Cape area, is also found in the high mountain kingdom of Lesotho, which is situated on a plateau 1000m/3200ft above sea level. In Dublin it makes a 2m/7ft curvaceous mound of fleshy blue-green leaves, with summer spires of lemon-yellow flowers with green tips, remarkably like those of *Kniphofia*. Somehow it's very satisfying to be able to grow a plant from tropical Africa in Dublin, which is at the same latitude as Newfoundland. The only attention this plant requires is two minutes' deadheading per year, and it needs a well-drained, sunny position.

Originally collected by Roy Lancaster on the slopes of Emei Shan in China, and later by Dan Hinkley of Heronswood Nursery, who generously gave me a plant, *Mahonia gracilipes* (1.5m/5ft) is a rare and beautiful shrub. On that magical, incredibly plant-rich mountain, I saw a specimen for myself, hanging from a shady cliff. (During that trip – it takes three days to go up and down – I was mugged by one of the large monkeys who live there. It leapt out from behind a monastery building and snatched the bag of biscuits I'd been eating. As in all the best smash and grabs, all was over before I realized what had happened.) The glossy dark, almost blue-green leaves of *M. gracilipes* have brilliantly contrasting powder-white backs to them. The leaf and flower stalks are light orange red, making a gorgeous midwinter picture, and the late-autumn flowers – similar to those of an epimedium (no surprise: both are members of the *Berberidaceae* family) – are pale red and yellow. Much to the liking of this mahonia, which is one of my most prized plants, it's growing

The lemon-yellow spires of *Aloe striatula* — miraculously easy from cuttings — with white diascia

in shade beside the front door, where the water barrel often overflows.

Another flower notable for being wonderful to the touch is the beautiful rosy-crimson waxy tubular bloom of Chilean *Philesia magellanica* (height 30cm/12in). Like those of *Lapageria*, to which it's closely related, the flowers feel deliciously cool. *Philesia* flowers are 5cm/2in in length, the leaves are leathery and evergreen, and the habit is dense. In my experience this needs acid soil (I have it in a small peat bed) and it doesn't bloom until its roots are so well established that they're all tangled together. Every year in autumn, it's a race between the slugs and me as to who gets to the flowers first.

The romantic side to gardening, as opposed to the strictly horticultural, is nicely illustrated in W.J. Bean's *Trees and Shrubs Hardy in the British Isles*: 'P. magellanica* was discovered by the French naturalist Philibert Commerson in the Magellan region . . . he was accompanied by his mistress Jeanne Baret, disguised as a manservant, and by the young Prince of Massau-Siegen. The charming generic name *Philesia* . . . comes from the Greek verb *philein*, to love . . .' The fact that its discoverer was christened Philibert, let alone everything else, is enough for me.

Buddleja agathosma (2m/7ft), given to me by Louisa Arbuthnott of Stone Cottage in Worcestershire, makes an amazing waterfall of palest silver grey in summer. Each leaf, toothed and wavy at the edges, has the texture of soft felt. In spring, on nearly bare branches (a few tatty leaves are still hanging on) there are pinky lavender fragrant small flowers. Planted against a warm wall, its roots by now very congested, this tender *Buddleja* makes a noticeable impact on the garden in summer. Val and I both think it is a wonderful shrub.

Potting shed

Tranquillity. Even saying the word has a calming effect. To me, the key to serenity is my shed. It has a lovely feeling of peace, and the good thing is that nobody knows exactly what I'm doing there. In reality I'm probably just standing still, gazing out of the window. But if footsteps approach I start banging pots about, hoping that whoever's coming along will think I'm too busy to be disturbed.

In January the shed has its annual spring clean. It takes courage to investigate the big wooden box of seed packets: row upon row of rattling packets, some never opened, others nameless. Here are seeds that I didn't sow last year, or the year before, or . . . Perhaps somebody I really like took a lot of trouble to post them and spent a lot on stamps. I never did like carrots, so why are there eleven different packets of carrot 'Early Nantes'? I must stop looking at the pretty pictures on the packets, stop my imagination running away, make a pile marked 'Sow soon', shut my eyes and dump the rest.

Since the last time the shed was tidied, things have built up. The problem is all the bits of wire, boxes, trays, screws, string, plant ties, blunt pencils, drying seedheads, nails rusty and shiny, bags paper and polythene, stakes with one end snapped off, paintbrushes solid with dry paint, bags of this and bottles of that – not enough to use but too good to throw away. You could write a thesis on the various hose connectors alone, in diverse metals and different-coloured plastic, all gathered in a large tin – thirty-six years of losing one's temper when the connector doesn't fit and rushing off to buy another one. (But never, of course, throwing the offending one away: it might come in useful.)

In winter, plants that need a frost-free rest, such as dahlias, cannas, tuberous begonias, *Rhodohypoxis* and summer-flowering *Gladioli*, are tucked up in peat here in trays or pots. If frost threatens, I can throw sacks or thick newspapers over the lot. Conversely, all the bulbs that need a dry, warm rest in summer, such as spring-flowering *Gladioli, Ixia, Sparaxis, Tecophilea* and *Tropaeolum azureum*, go to the shed as soon as their leaves have died off around May. (Incidentally, I usually sprinkle stored dahlia tubers with water once a month in January and February to stop them shrivelling. And cannas should not be allowed to get too dry or they will take time to recover.)

I love the definition of the verb 'to potter' in my *Chambers Dictionary* – 'to busy oneself in a desultory way: to dawdle'. Yes, one of the secrets of life is a good shed.

Roses I still grow

How could I possibly make the same mistake again? Three times I've been taken in by seeing rose 'New Dawn' (3m/10ft) looking adorable, a mass of pale pink, scented flowers. I've ordered it immediately, planted it with hope, longed for the buds to open and spent August picking up fallen petals. But by September there'd be scarcely a leaf left. They'd all be on the ground, displaying the tell-tale blotches of blackspot. However, in places with hotter summers than ours, such as East Coast USA, I've seen wonderful examples of healthy 'New Dawn' with masses of clean, undamaged foliage.

Another rose, one of my favourite big pink cabbage-type roses, climbing Hybrid Tea 'Madame Grégoire Staechelin' (4m/12ft), by late summer had an embarrassing lack of leaves. Lovely as they were, both roses went to the great rose garden in the sky. But, welcome to stay on is rose 'Climbing Caroline Testout' (4m/12ft), which has silvery pink flowers of the cabbagey sort, usually seen on Ascot hats and birthday cards. Blackspot isn't too bad, and there's a second flush of September flowers to anticipate.

In pictures, rose 'Félicité Parmentier' (90cm/3ft or slightly more) looks highly desirable: the full flowers an even more sensitive pink than the above. But in our damp Irish climate the flowers rarely open properly because of 'balling': if it rains as the flower is opening the outer petals become soggy and cling together, so the bud can't open. We rarely saw a perfect bloom. Then there was the desperately fragile 'La France', the first-ever Hybrid Tea, bred in 1867 (90cm/3ft), and poor 'Madame Hardy' (1.5m/5ft), an old double white rose with a fetching green middle, which lived in the rain shadow of next door's yew. All these had to go.

However, we have kept an even more troublesome rose, namely 'Louis XIV'. This rose won't tolerate a drop of moisture on the buds or flowers, which instantly shrivel and go brown. With us this never grows more than 60cm/24in (perhaps weakened by the excesses of its namesake, the Sun King), so we grow it in a pot, which stays outside the door to the greenhouse so that we can drag it in when the buds are forming. As one of the China roses, 'Louis XIV' has the merit of repeat flowering. The buds are silky black and the flowers are a luscious, sultry, deep, dark red.

I've never taken out any of the Hybrid Musk roses. They are such brilliant garden plants. We grow 'Buff Beauty' (1.5m/5ft), clusters of soft apricot-yellow flowers; 'Cornelia' (1.5m/5ft), pink deepening in the centre of the flower, light apricot flush, here for thirty years; 'Prosperity' (1.5m/5ft), double, creamy-white, particularly good in autumn. There are so many excellent Hybrid Musks, all with sunny natures and healthy foliage. (I keep meaning to get 'Penelope' (1.5m/5ft) – very floriferous, pale pink.)

Rose 'Rhapsody in Blue' does well in a large pot.

The rose we call 'Bengal Crimson' (I think it is listed in the *RHS Plant Finder* as *Rosa* x *odorata* Sanguinea Group 'Bengal Crimson') is an uncommon China rose, with gorgeous large floppy-petalled single flowers, to 1.5m/5ft, but taller against a warm wall. This came from Rosemary Brown, who has a wonderful garden, Graigueconna, near Bray, County Wicklow. In mild winters it puts on a special Christmas show. I adore this rose and have planted a young specimen on the south-east-facing wall of the mews, where it should reach double the height. Making a beautiful alliance, it has intermingled with *Salvia involucrata* 'Bethellii' (1.5m/5ft) and looks good, as they are similar shades of magenta pink.

Another uncommon rose here in Ireland is 'Général Schablikine' (1.5m/5ft). Its virtues were sung in 1898 in a book by Lord Brougham on the roses at Château Eleonore, in Cannes: 'If a law was passed that one man should cultivate but one variety of rose, I should without hesitation choose 'Général Schablikine'.' Its fragrant flowers are soft, coppery pink, very double and old-fashioned looking. As a Tea rose, it is on the tender side, but it has the advantage of an extremely long blooming season.

My relationship with roses runs hot and cold. They are difficult to incorporate into contemporary planting. Their pests and diseases are a nuisance. When I'm weeding near by, prickly branches grab me. When I'm deadheading, thorns get down the side of my thumbs. But when in early summer roses are in the first bloom of youth, and I see some new ones, I'm charmed all over again. Out comes the notebook and pen – consider it ordered.

Moss rose 'William Lobb' (2.5m/8ft), dating from 1855, was a special favourite of the renowned Irish dress designer Sybil Connolly. I love this rose, not least for its mossy buds, each one covered in bright green chenille, but the semi-double flowers are a magical mix of colours, which change as the flowers mature, of mulberry purple, lilac pink and lavender grey. There's only one early summer flush of flowers on 'William Lobb', but the foliage is cleaner and a better green than that of other old roses. Pruning is easy. You can prune it to 60cm/2ft or 2.5m/8ft – I've done both. You can prune it after flowering, midwinter, the following spring or not at all.

'William Lobb' makes me think of a modern rose with similar colouring that I absolutely adore, 'Rhapsody in Blue' (1–3m/3–10ft). This is a repeat bloomer, with a delicious scent, better than most antique snob-value roses named after a French princess, duke or duchess. The flowers are dark purple blue, the reverse of the petals deep amethyst.

Here this grows in a large pot on the terrace and is also being trained to the wall of the mews. Many climbing roses are just too vigorous for smaller gardens, but Hybrid Musks, such as 'Prosperity' or 'Cornelia', are very amenable to being turned into small climbers, for training to trellis, arches and low walls.

'Eden Rose 88' (also more romantically known as 'Pierre de Ronsard'), another modern rose, grows to about 2.5m/8ft on the arches, just the sort of height we want. The flowers are lemony cream, the edges of the petals flushed pink at the edges, voluptuously wrapped around each other. I can almost see this rose mincing into a bar, wearing a feather boa and peep-toe shoes. Near neighbour is 'Bonica' (90cm/3ft), a much more suburban cultivar, but undeniably generous with flowers of a slightly common pink. Hyacinth Bucket would love it.

Whenever I see 'Duchesse de Brabant' (90cm/3ft) I think of the rosy pink of the little shells you pick up on Irish and English beaches. Another vision is of a humid afternoon in a cemetery in Richmond, Virginia, where, searching for graves with the family name of my great-grandmother (I've since discovered that she came from Rhode Island), I saw this rose, with its beautifully cupped fragrant flowers, and took a cutting. It lives on the terrace in a pot. We scoop away about 10cm/4in of the surface of the potting mixture in early spring and replace it with fresh mix, and every few years repot completely, pruning the roots as well as the branches as we do so. Use a soil-based potting compost.

You can't accuse me of being fickle, as my favourite rose, despite its fastidious ways, is still 'Souvenir du Docteur Jamain' (2.5m/8ft), introduced in about 1865. You rarely have more than one or two perfect blooms at once, as both sun and rain quickly ruin them. But for such sumptuous shades of deep red, and perfume for which one deep breath is never enough, I'd take this rose before all others. Having said that, our old specimen of this has recently succumbed to ongoing weakness. Next time we'll try it in a large pot on the terrace.

On the other hand, rose 'Charles de Mills' (1.5m/5ft) has its flowers all in one glorious show, but only once a year. Each bloom has great beauty, the petals so tightly packed together that they form luxurious crimson swirls, shaded deep blackcurrant in the crevices between. This is pruned immediately after flowering, as there's no point in leaving a whole lot of growth, which can shade nearby plants, when there are going to be no more flowers until the following year.

An old Irish rose, 'Souvenir de Saint Anne's' (1.5m/5ft) arose around 1900 as a sport from 'Souvenir de la Malmaison' on the north side of Dublin in the garden of Lady Ardilaun, who refused to part with a cutting unless the beneficiary promised not to give it away. This lovely pale pink long-flowering rose would never have survived had it not been looked after by Lady (Phylis) Moore, wife of the then director of the Botanic Gardens at Glasnevin. She eventually gave it to Graham Stuart Thomas, who distributed it in the 1950s to the nursery trade.

Lady Ardilaun was neatly repaid for being so mean by Miss Ellen Willmott (1858–1934), the celebrated English gardener who, after a visit to the garden at St Anne's, remarked in a letter that she 'was surprised how very little [Lady Ardilaun] knew about plants and gardening'. She added, 'She told me that her garden was quite wonderful', but concluded: 'Whatever be the case it is most fortunate that the owner is so completely satisfied.'

Water

Water has a strange and wonderful effect on the garden. Here, taking out the lawn and replacing it with a canal released a whole new range of sensations. Wind and sunlight play on the water's surface; one minute you have little sparkly light-catching waves, which can't decide which way they're going, and the next all is mysterious and still. And I love the canal when a storm flashes over it and rain tosses it into sheets of silvery rippling water.

Watching water has a hypnotic effect: reflections appear to have an extra dimension, and you see things that aren't really there. At night we have the strange spectacle of the long dark mirror of the canal, glassy still, throwing back an image of the lights in the hall lantern. Standing in the garden, people see the reflections but not the lights themselves (an odd phenomenon: because it's so long the canal can 'see' what's on the ceilings in the house, whereas we can't). By day, puffy white clouds floating on a blue sky are mirrored in the water, winter sun glows pink in the west, storm clouds pile up, the moon rises and if so much as a seagull flies over the canal you can see its twin go by in the water.

I'm often asked why we don't have plants in the canal – and why there are no goldfish. But I want water for water's sake, rather as it's revered in hot countries, where it cools and irrigates, calms and refreshes. There are several different levels, and there are plants in the lowest pool that I much enjoy as vertical contrast: irises (we have a pale yellow form of *Iris pseudacorus*, 1.2m/4ft), bulrushes (*Typha angustifolia*, 2m/7ft) and horsetails (*Equisetum hyemale*, 1.5m/5ft), which I grow in a pot in case it gets out and tries to colonize Dublin.

For me a water feature – what it looks like and where it is positioned – has to be entirely credible. Obviously man-made expanses of water look right near buildings, but out in the country an informal pool looks as if it belongs – provided there's no suspicion of pond liner to be seen. I have a problem with preformed pools, with their unnaturally wiggly edges, and I don't think ponds look as if they belong in front gardens generally; and as for ponds on the tops of slopes . . .

In the seven years since we first installed the canal, a world of tiny creatures has arrived. These busy themselves at the bottom of the pool, keeping the water sweet and clear. Bees are mesmerized by the water and are always falling in and having to be rescued with a leaf turned into a raft. The same mallard ducks visit every year in the courting season from March until the end of June.

I've been experimenting with water in the garden for thirty-six years, during which I've made every mistake that could possibly be made. I've tried cement pools, lined pools and reinforced concrete pools. They've been dug out and filled in again. They've turned slimy and gooey with mud. Blanket weed and ducks have moved in. I've bought pumps – powerful ones for Versailles-style jets, small ones with oh-so-dainty squirts. There's been too much light, so algae has turned the water green, or oxygenating plants have multiplied too fast, so that the water looks more like a bog than a pool.

The tall jet of water was my first mistake. The water shot straight into the air and smashed down with a terrible noise like the sea crashing into caves. Everywhere around was puddled and flooded, and the pool was nearly empty. End of that experiment. Next we tried the gentle spray. Too mean a trickle. You may have to try various pumps and sprays to get it right. The sound of water should soothe rather than irritate, and not make you want to visit the bathroom. The canal here has three small waterfalls with a circulating pump under the terrace. Peter McGarry, who with John and Fran built the canal, says that it's better built than his house: reinforced concrete to start with, then heavy-duty liner, which has been plastered to conceal it.

On a small scale, one of my more successful attempts at water gardening took many years to evolve. In about 1985 I suddenly got annoyed with one of the small, muddy, rectangular pools (in the hidden little paved garden up on the right) and took it to bits. But still standing in the middle of the paving was the nineteenth-century lead statue in the form of a cherub, about 1.5m/5ft tall, all rounded cheeks and curly hair. So in 1986 (New Year's Day, to be precise) I went to Killiney beach, about thirty minutes' drive away, and picked up several buckets of pebbles (you're not allowed to do that these days). I wanted to make a circular pebble mosaic surround for the statue.

In the early 1990s we took up the pebble mosaic (but I'm going to try another one elsewhere) around the statue and a good plumber made a galvanized iron underground tank, which we installed under the statue. The tank is 1.5m/5ft wide and 1m/3ft deep, with the top in eight different sections, easy to lift, like wedges of a cake, with lots of small holes about 8mm/⅓in wide. A small pump lives in the tank for recirculating the water and a ballcock to top up the level if it ever goes too low. The tank is completely disguised by a layer (10cm/4in deep) of grey pea gravel. If I ever need to get at the pump, which isn't often, I simply scrape away the gravel, lift up one of the wedge-shaped pieces of the lid of the tank and have immediate access. The excellent thing about the whole arrangement is that the pea gravel acts as a non-stop filter, so the water stays remarkably clean.

Soon afterwards we planted a dwarf box hedge in the form of a square as an edge to this. We used *Buxus sempervirens* 'Suffruticosa', which I believe is the only box cultivar content to be kept as a very low hedge (25cm/10in).

Although I never thought I'd get bored with the hedge as well, soon out it came, to be replaced by a simplified surface of raked gravel. Finally, last spring, I took against the cherub himself, deciding he was too twee. He now lives in the basement, on his way to auction.

You've probably heard the saying 'Statues are simply the gnomes of the upper classes.' Neither I nor anybody else has the right to criticize other people's choice of garden ornament. Still, the snob in me has to admit that it was in 2004 at the Atlanta Flower Show when I saw a stand with rows of cherubs identical to mine, all reproduction, that I sort of went off him. Anyway, I always feel that on your way around a garden, if you come face to face with something that seems to be saying 'Hi, look at me – I'm your garden feature' then it's time for it to go.

I really like his replacement, an early octagonal marble font given to us by a friend, Jimmy O'Donnell, who in turn was given it by the warden of a small church (St Kevin's in Glendalough), where it had been thrown out (it had probably been replaced

In a climate like ours, with low light intensity, water pulls the sky down to earth. And the canal centres the eye on the middle of the garden. You can just see the blossom on the large Bramley apple at the end on the left. The pale pink tulips are 'Angélique' and 'Apricot Beauty'.

The small marble font is popular with small birds.

with a modern font). There is a low water spout, with a gentle trickle, constantly visited by small birds, including long-tailed tits and goldcrests, which hide in the dense evergreen leaves of a nearby sarcococca.

Note for laying pebble mosaic: first have a plan in your head about what sort of pattern you're making. Have all the pebbles you need to hand and aim to do only what you can finish that day. Thin, flattish, smooth, oval stones are the best, roughly 5cm/2in long. These stay in better than rounded stones, which are inclined to pop out again. Level the area. Lay a damp, but not wet, mix of 3 parts sand and 1 part cement over the area you're going to do. Place your pebbles in this, a bit proud, on their sides (edge) rather than flat. Bury to nearly half their depth. Lay a board over them and tap it down gently. Make a 5:1 dry mix of sand and cement and sprinkle it over thinly. Very lightly brush with a soft brush. Sprinkle with water, using a fine rose on the watering can. Cover with a sheet of polythene and weigh it down with stones around the edge of the mosaic. Don't tread on the mosaic for at least one month while it sets really firm.

Pruning

Let's be quite clear: flying into a rage and cutting back a shrub that's overgrown its allotted space is called hacking (although you won't see the 'h' word listed in the indexes of garden books). People think that pruning is something a shrub requires as a right, just like water. You can almost hear gardeners muttering, 'It obviously needs a good prune', as they set off armed with secateurs and saw.

I'll never forget how, while out shopping one day, I rounded a corner to see a man in the process of slaughtering a hedge of privet. He must have known he was guilty, as before each chop of the shears he looked furtively right and left, eyes narrowed to a slit. (It must be his cousin who gardens near here in communal gardens, apartment blocks and public lavatories, where every shrub is clipped tightly into a uniform blob.)

Agreed, the longer a garden has been in existence, the more adjusting must be done to allow each plant enough light and space. Still, if you can't sort out the balance between two shrubs growing side by side by taking off, after careful consideration, a branch or two, it might be better to remove one of the plants altogether. You're only going to meet the same problem – only worse – next year. Of course there are shrubs that come to no harm, and grow happily entwined, leaning on each other for support like an elderly married couple.

Even buddlejas don't actually *need* pruning; it's just that we gardeners don't like looking at a great lanky shrub, with the flowers and attendant butterflies way up in the air. Some buddlejas flower on the current season's wood, so *B. davidii* (3m/10ft) is hard pruned in late winter to 90cm/3ft. Other shrubs that bloom on the wood made the same year are treated the same way, such as *Ceanothus* x *delileanus* (5m/16ft) and *Hydrangea paniculata* (4m/12ft), caryopteris, ceratostigma and lavatera. With early-spring-blooming shrubs such as *Jasminum nudiflorum* (3m/10ft), flowering shoots are taken off as soon as blossoms fade. Tender shrubs have frost-damaged shoots removed in spring. The rule for early-summer-flowering shrubs, such as weigelas, deutzias and philadelphus, is to cut away weak growth and some of the just-flowered shoots straight after blooming, to give space to young shoots for next year. *Akebia quinata*, a vanilla-scented and chocolate-flowered fast climber on one of the arches here, must be cut back to 2m/7ft each autumn, or else it will swamp all around it.

As a general rule with all shrubs and trees, take out dead, diseased, damaged or weak wood. I often think of the story about the doyenne of Irish gardening who kept her secateurs beside her knife and fork at lunchtime. On an extended post-lunch tour round the garden, she'd stand beside every shrub she met, making a great performance of taking a nip here and a tuck there.

With roses, the rule is that weak branches are hard pruned or removed completely; very old woody stems are cut to the base occasionally; vigorous young stems are encouraged. We cut back many roses in late autumn as part of the general autumn tidy. By then they are top-heavy and subject to wind rock, and the weight of the branches needs to be reduced anyway. We try to pick up all fallen rose leaves to prevent recycling blackspot disease for another year.

We have another look at the rose bushes in early spring, perhaps taking out any remaining weak growth and checking which way the buds are pointing. The aim is to cut just above an outward-facing bud. (This means that when the rose begins to grow the new branch is heading away from the bush, thus preventing congestion in the centre and ensuring more air movement and less blackspot.) Tea roses (such as 'Climbing Lady Hillingdon') dislike hard pruning, and we also go lightly on Hybrid Musks and Chinas, just taking away thin twiggy bits and topping the better branches by a few centimetres. With Hybrid Teas and Floribundas, I might or might not prune them hard. Much depends on whereabouts in the border they are – perhaps they must be tall to compete with neighbouring plants, or I may need them shorter if they are in the front.

When you buy a climbing rose, be sure to keep the label so that you can look it up to check whether it's a Climber or a Rambler. For Climbers, reduce the shoots by two-thirds in spring, but leave the main framework alone. When deadheading after flowering, reduce flowering shoots by half. With Ramblers (such as 'Dorothy Perkins', which I used to grow before I realized how prone it was to mildew), the flowering shoots can be removed as soon as they've faded, and the young shoots tied in. If there aren't enough of these, keep a few of the old ones.

When training roses to walls or trellises, it's useful to remember that what the rose wants is to get quickly to the top of the support and then bloom, providing one flower (or cluster of flowers) from each stem. But your aim is to force the stem to produce as many flowers as possible. By tying in the stem horizontally, rather than vertically, you force the rose to produce a new bud, and thus an extra lot of flowers, at each leaf joint, thus presenting a mass of colour rather than a singleton. That's why it's important to have your walls well equipped with supporting wires to tie the rose branches to.

One thing I've noticed from visiting the USA is how well trees are limbed up there. Shade gardens are much needed in the hotter summers, and tall trees casting shade from high above have their lower branches cleanly removed, creating space for underplanting. In this garden *Cornus mas*

'Variegata' (5m/16ft), the cornelian cherry, has been pruned up, and many of the lower branches, plus the side branches of those

higher up, have been cut away. Thus this lovely early-flowering shrub, with tiny lemon-yellow flowers wreathing the branches in March, is much more airy looking in summer. Underneath there's enough light for peonies, hostas, Solomon's seals and hellebores. *Acer griseum* (12m/40ft) in the red border and *Caragana arborescens* 'Lorbergii' (6m/20ft) in the small paved area have been similarly treated.

Deadheading

Deadheading is most unfashionable at the moment, but I love it. It's not very strenuous, and gives lots of excuses for standing around. Deadheading is done for several reasons: to encourage a plant to make more flowers; to stop it losing energy by forming unnecessary seed; and to prevent it becoming a weed by incontinent self-seeding. But my primary reason for deadheading is that certain plants after flowering look plain ugly unless deadheaded and tidied up and I don't wish to be reminded that in the midst of life we're in death.

Sometimes, with plants such as sweet peas, there's a big decision to make. If I don't cut off the flowers, the plant will rapidly go to seed. Should we have the pleasure of flowers this very evening, which look and smell heavenly, or should we snip them off for the sake of later gratification? Should we spend our youth and money all in one go, in and out of the pubs and clubs – having it all now – or save up for a comfortable middle age? You can never have everything. If you pick flowers for the house, you haven't got the colour outdoors. But still, the more you pick your sweet peas, the more they'll produce.

Deadheading may not be all that fashionable a concept. The beauty of plants that have gone to seed is now justly recognized. But a great mass of large pink blooms on something like a camellia is ruined for me if there are browning petals and dead flowers all mixed up with them. I was actually quite pleased when our fremontodendron, a Californian shrub, suddenly collapsed and died. The lovely yellow saucer flowers were completely spoilt by dead flowers hanging on.

If the roses aren't deadheaded, the garden looks unkempt as opposed to romantic. It's no use wittering on about how lovely rosehips are. They are indeed. But here we check over roses in general (except those grown for hips) nearly every day in summer. Sometimes I just snatch off dead flowers while talking to somebody, but mostly we do it properly: using sharp secateurs, make a clean cut just above the second or third leaf below the deadhead; if the stem is weak, take it off to healthy growth lower down.

All our efforts from spring on are about keeping the show going. Starting with daffodils: after flowering the bulb leaves are busy building up the bulb for next year, so we take off only the faded flower using finger and thumb, leaving the stalk to help the leaves with their work. Our few rhododendrons have their clusters of green seedheads snapped off the moment they form. (It's no use removing them later when they're brown as the plant's energy is already wasted by then.)

In early summer we pick off the flowers of the peach-leaved bellflower (*Campanula persicifolia*, 60cm/24in) individually to promote further buds. Eventually I feel the plant has made such a valiant effort that it's time to cut the flowering stem back to the basal rosette of leaves. We also remove the single flowers of aquilegias or colum-

Deadheading galega

bines and they continue to produce young ones until I decide, some time in May or early June, that enough's enough and cut the flower stems and leaves (tatty by now) to the ground. The plant quickly renews itself. We remove the faded central spires of delphiniums and foxgloves so that the flowers developing on side shoots will be better displayed. Brunneras look wrecked after flowering, their old stems covered in greenfly and their leaves droopy. We chop the whole plant to ground level and give it a good soak of water. Astrantias bloom for a long time from May. Dark red cultivars, such as *Astrantia major* 'Ruby Wedding' (75cm/30in), look good long after the flowers have faded, but if you allow seed to drop, inferior forms turn up. We cut the flowering stems back to the base, plus any dead leaves in late June; a fresh crop of flowers arrives in September. All summer I fiddle about nipping off old flowers of pansies and violas until their stems sprawl too much, when I chop them down to about 3cm/1in.

Later in the summer we used to find galega worthwhile, with its pretty clouds of mauve and white flowers like little lupins, looking good for six weeks. But the clumps took half an hour each week to deadhead. As Shirley Conran said in the 1960s, 'Life's too short to stuff a mushroom,' so out they came.

Argyranthemums (tender perennials related to chrysanthemums with a long flowering season) bloom for months in summer. We prune single deadheads, of both flower and stem, back to stronger growth (about 10cm/4in). They get a major prune (with about 15cm/6in cut off each stalk) around late July. After a few weeks' rest, they flower again until frost. We also individually deadhead the scabious-like crimson flowers of *Knautia macedonica* (60cm/24in). This year I'm going to try cutting the plants to ground level in July to make them more compact.

We give dahlias as much attention with the secateurs as the roses. The flowers of some are beautifully formed when they first open, but when overblown seem passé, even before petal-fall. Cut off the faded bloom and stalk together, just above a leaf. In early autumn the secateurs are also very busy with annual cosmos and salvias.

Another excellent method of prolonging the display of certain perennials is to cut back the tips of the stems (just the growing point, the top 5cm/2in or so) well before flowering, when the plants are in full growth in summer. So treated, the stems flower later in the season. This works particularly well with border phlox: we cut back half of each clump and the other half flowers at the usual time, creating a two-tiered effect. We do the normal deadheading as usual as well as this, by removing the central flower cluster as it fades, thus encouraging lateral shoots to form and flower. Phloxes work hard in this garden. Many other perennials (such as asters and eupatoriums) respond well to chopping back or pinching out the tops of the leafy stems.

I deadhead lots of plants as I pass by, with finger and thumb – single dead flowers of hemerocallis and dianthus, for instance. With alstroemerias you firmly grab the dead head, still attached to its 90cm/3ft stem, and yank the whole thing out from the roots. The plants don't appear to mind. *Alchemilla mollis* (45cm/18in) seeds everywhere if you don't chop the whole thing to the ground, leaves and all, soon after flowering and before it sets seed. Difficult to do, because it looks quite nice and it seems a shame to cut it. Fresh new leaves will rapidly turn up.

PUTTING MANNERS ON THE GARDEN

A significant contribution to how this garden looks happens at the same time as the deadheading: this is the polish, the bit extra. This makes the essential difference between the garden looking only fine or really terrific. It includes tweaking away a leaf covered in blackspot, the slug-eaten bit of acanthus, the fallen leaves of a bay tree; cleaning out dead phormium, astelia or celmisia leaves, using scissors (the stiff leaves of these plants, all from New Zealand, often snag if you use secateurs for the job); spending ten minutes on one dierama, again using scissors, and removing unsightly faded foliage; scuffling up footprints in the flowerbed; remembering to cut out the old stems of bamboo, to fully expose the beauty of the new ones, or taking out the old wood of a shrub to let in light and air; and finally getting round to cutting off that bit of pyracantha that jabs me every time I pass by. Only by actually being in contact with plants – as when deadheading or weeding – do these small tasks present themselves.

The Mediterranean garden

I can't bear to see plants fainting from lack of water. We are forever rushing around with reviving cans for phlox, clematis and delphiniums. I like these plants too much to give them up, but more and more I'm noticing that the happiest plants here are those classified as 'Mediterranean', although under this heading, used climatically as well as geographically, you could find mimosa and eucalyptus from Australia, cestrum and puyas from South America, as well as typical Mediterranean plants such as rosemary, lavender and cistus.

When I first acquired *Agave parryi* (rosettes 45–75cm/18–30in), from the south-east of the USA and Mexico, I couldn't believe that it was hardy outdoors, but it has thrived here, not a bother on it as they say, for nearly thirty years. The fleshy, glaucous, exceedingly spiky leaves form a decorative rosette on a raised bed in full sun. Better still is the super form *Agave parryi* var. *parryi* (45cm/18in) which is more compact, with wider, pale blue leaves. For me, the singular beauty of agaves is the wavy pattern imprinted on the leaves, called ghosting, caused by the young leaves being closely furled around each other in the middle of the rosette.

It's not our Irish frost that will kill the agaves but too much rain, so I prepared exceedingly well-drained planting holes for them, mostly consisting of rubble, broken brick and gravel. Instead of sticking to normal rules – that is, planting at the same level exactly as the agaves were in their pots – I set them a few centimetres proud of their surrounds. I piled up the resulting spaces with gravel.

I planted a spiky Mexican plant, with a wonderfully musical, mellifluous name, dasylirion (I think mine is *D. acrotrichum*, 1.2m/4ft), in the same way in a hot sunny bed beside the greenhouse. Now there's a perfectly symmetrical 90cm/3ft dome of barbed leaves, each prettily frayed pale biscuit at the tips. I used to make a polythene hat to protect it from winter rain, but it invariably blew away, so it's now risking life without protection.

Hot, dry conditions and poor soil are perfectly acceptable for a tall leguminous shrub, *Cytisus battandieri* (5m/16ft), from the mountains of Morocco, with silky, silver, laburnum-like leaves, satin to the touch, and flowers like yellow lupins scented of pineapple. Its only fault is that it becomes top-heavy and rocks at the roots in wind, so it's best planted against a wall, tied in firmly

Spiky *Dasylirion acrotrichum* with rosemary, salvias and species gladioli survive well without extra water. The small red flowers to the right are rhodohypoxis.

and regularly pruned by removing old growths after flowering and tipping the smaller branches.

I must tell you about a really good shrub, *Cestrum parqui* (4m/12ft). In colder climates this behaves like a herbaceous perennial (coming up and flowering from the ground each year). It is very resilient: my bush is twenty years old and thrives in poor dry soil against a wall facing east. The leaves stink when crushed and the flowers smell horrid by day. Apart from a very long flowering season, with non-stop production of pretty lime-yellow flowers, there's a delicious surprise awaiting you at midnight: the rank smell of the flowers is magically transformed (darkness must be total or else it won't happen) into a sweet and languorous perfume, all for the benefit of passing moths, which pollinate the willow-leaved jessamine, a Chilean plant. We usually prune this in winter to about 2m/7ft, but in fact you can cut it back or not – however it suits you and your garden.

If I was a making a garden totally out of drought-tolerant plants, I'd begin with a group of myrtles (*Myrtus communis*, 5m/16ft) for their shiny evergreen leaves and refreshing white flowers in August, with cream stamens in the middle. My specimen thrives in an exceptionally dry corner. You can prune a myrtle as much or as little as you like. I cut mine back after flowering, but in colder climates spring pruning would be advisable.

I'd plant plenty of *Euphorbia characias* subsp. *wulfenii* (1.5m/5ft). I never tire of this well-known shrub's blue-green leaves and large, bright lime-yellow long-lasting flowerheads (it is known as frogspawn plant here in Dublin). Try to get a really good cultivar, such as 'Jimmy Platt', 'Lambrook Gold' or 'John Tomlinson'. Two minutes' care per year per plant is all these require. In early summer the flowering stems (which have been doing their stuff for at least four months) will start looking tired. You must cut these back to the base (don't forget about the allergic properties of the white sap – wear gloves).

Then I'd plant all the herbs that love hot dry places – lavender, rosemary, thyme, santolina and different origanums, with masses of fennel (*Foeniculum vulgare*, 90cm/3ft) for its fluffy delicate texture as well as giant fennel (*Ferula communis*, 2.5m/8ft). This is one of the biggest umbellifers (plants with flowers the same shape as cow parsley or Queen Anne's lace), a

Solanum jasminoides 'Album' can be pruned to 90cm/3ft in spring if required.

highly ornamental addition to the garden when in bloom. I'd have lots of different grasses: giant oats (*Stipa gigantea*, 1.5m/5ft), common as it is, I would plant with the sun behind it, and for later in the season there'd be many miscanthus and pennisetums. *Choisya ternata* (2m/7ft), bay, sarcococca, box, aucuba and fatsia would live in the shade of the Irish native strawberry tree (*Arbutus unedo*, 10m/33ft). Grey and silver plants (see page 117) would be there in abundance. Buddlejas, *Bupleurum fruticosum* (3m/10ft), Californian lilacs (ceanothus) and New Zealand cabbage trees (*Cordyline australis*, 10m/33ft) would provide extra height.

Pachystegia insignis 'Minor' (90cm/3ft), a shrubby New Zealand grey-leaved plant with stiff leathery leaves and fresh white daisy flowers, thrived here for fifteen years in a hot dry place. Lastly, a mention for the heavenly or sacred bamboo (*Nandina domestica*, 2m/7ft). This has elegant evergreen leaves (each made up of lots of smaller leaves), red flushed when young, ageing to green, and tiny flowers followed by shiny red berries. Worth a bucketful of compliments, it doesn't seem to mind where you position it and it requires nothing whatsoever by way of care. Just remember, occasionally, to remind yourself what an excellent plant it is.

This is just the beginning of a vast list of plants suitable for a dry sunny garden with no extra watering. What about the climbers? (I'd start with *Solanum laxum* 'Album'.)

I often find that the best rain spell is to lug umpteen watering cans round the garden. Raindrops will arrive at that very moment when you finally stop and sit down.

Scent

I love the damp, warm, slightly peppery smell of a greenhouse full of plants. The windows are steamy; droplets of water run down the inside of the glass. Plants hustle for space. Leaves adjust themselves for the best angle to catch the most light. I usually begin a tour of the garden by going into my greenhouse, not only to check on the plants but also to breathe the earthy, humid, comforting aroma peculiar to greenhouses.

Scents in the garden are sometimes so elusive that the moment you look for them, they disappear. Floating round the garden in early spring, when you least expect to meet them, are waves of warm vanilla from azara and sweet box or sarcococca. Later in the season intense perfumes such as that of lilies are so alluring to the nose that you can't pass by without granting their flowers a deep sniff, thus getting yourself covered in pollen for your trouble. We are so bombarded with chemical scents, all day every day, whether we're cleaning the bath or eating a strawberry yoghurt, that I have to keep reminding myself that all the delicious garden smells are actually real: from flowers and pungent aromatic leaves and earth warmed by sun after rain to the sweet, hay-like scents of autumn.

My first choice for a shrub to plant near the front or back door, so that you can't leave the house without inhaling its scent in winter, would be *Daphne bholua* (3m/10ft), a shrub from the Himalayas. It has purply pink flowers and leathery, dullish evergreen leaves. The midwinter scent is so thrilling that I feel quite giddy. On mild days walking round the garden you keep meeting delicious wafts. My specimen is elderly, about twenty, and lives against a sheltered wall. Occasionally, I pot up or transplant suckers from the base and I prune away any tired old wood after flowering.

Coronilla valentina subsp. *glauca* 'Citrina' (1.5m/5ft) is a lovely small shrub for a warm wall and excellent in a pot, with delicate blue-green leaves and pale lemon-yellow flowers for most of the year, especially in winter. The elusive fragrance has been described as peachy – I wouldn't know what to call it but it certainly smells nice.

Jasminum polyanthum (climber) grew for years in the border of the greenhouse, where its clusters of white jasmine flowers dispensed heavenly spring scent. I then realized that it was hardy

Coronilla valentina subsp. *glauca* 'Citrina' in early April, with *Arum creticum*

here and moved it outdoors to a sheltered wall. Flowering is later outside and the buds are flushed deep pink. This makes an excellent spring-flowering house plant. Vigorous and easily renewed by cuttings or layering, under glass it should be hard pruned after flowering.

Flowers that always make me go back for a second sniff are the light orange wallflowers of *Erysimum* 'Dawn Breaker' (40cm/16in), an indispensable small shrub with a powerful scent; rose 'Souvenir du Docteur Jamain' and tender *Rhododendron* 'Lady Alice Fitzwilliam' (1.5m/5ft), which grows in the shady peat bed in front of the house.

Aloysia triphylla (3m/10ft), the lemon-scented verbena from Chile and Argentina, has unexciting leaves and deeply insignificant small flowers. But to pick, crush and sniff a leaf is to get a wonderfully reviving, strong lemony scent that I'd hate to be without. It's no beauty, and one doesn't need a lot of it. I prune mine to about 1.5m/5ft in spring. It's not fussy about soil and likes sun, good drainage and the protection of a wall. You can also grow it in a big pot.

Muscari macrocarpum (15cm/6in) is a hardy bulb. I find it flowers better if pot grown and dried off between the end of May and early September, when the bulbs are repotted and started into growth. Unless the weather's very cold, the pot remains outdoors until buds form, when I move it

into the unheated alpine house. The flowers are purple-grey in bud, opening to yellow, with a knockout fragrance.

One of my more successful experiments with the making of standards (a ball-on-a-stick affair) has been with the woodbine or honeysuckle *Lonicera periclymenum* 'Graham Thomas' (twining to 4m/12ft). When I grew this free range, it tried to strangle its neighbours and went everywhere, but grown as a standard, and trained on to a metal shape like an upside-down hanging basket, it was a success. I planted it beside the front gate, and every time we came home late at night there was a heavenly all-pervading scent.

To make a standard honeysuckle: root three cuttings in a pot; don't pinch out the top of each cutting to let them grow tall, and tie each to an individual cane; when they are about 60–90cm/2–3ft high, plait or twine the stems around each other. At all times keep the stem of your standard tied firmly to its support. Except for the main growths forming the shape of the 'head', keep the remaining shoots well pruned, especially after flowering. The great value of growing honeysuckle like this is that you get an incredibly high ratio of marvellous scent compared to the small (90cm/3ft square) amount of ground the plant occupies. The idea came from a visit to an artist's garden in Wales.

ABOVE Rose 'Souvenir du Docteur Jamain'
BELOW *Daphne bholua*

Hiding the neighbours

For the first time in six years we've washed the white net curtains in the living room. The contrast between deep grey 'before' and Persil-white 'after' is spectacular. But most of us don't have time to spy on the neighbours (here we only keep the net curtains to protect the real curtains, which are too expensive to replace) and I'm far too busy to care who looks in at the windows. I feel the same when I'm in the garden. As I said earlier, what matters to me more than anything is light.

The deeply rooted desire to possess land is present in all of us. To secure this land, most of us behave like two dogs in an alley, and I never stop hearing of arguments over the position of boundaries, high walls built over long August weekends, overhanging branches, party hedges taken out when neighbours were on holiday and decades of ill feeling to do with the taking of somebody else's sunlight – not to mention hedges of x *Cupressocyparis leylandii*.

The other day I was discussing with a garden visitor a newly built bungalow that had just appeared over the wall at the end of her garden. It was occupied, she informed me, by 'two CSs' (which means apparently 'two Cream Sofas' – two trendy people with minimalist taste). Anyway, there it was, and from morning till night, she couldn't look out of any window at the back of the house without seeing this blot on her own particular landscape. What could she do?

'Thirty metres, facing south,' she replied, when I asked how long the garden was, and what aspect it had. I suggested she sacrificed 4–5m/12–16ft of length for a belt of woodland of native plants such as hazel (*Corylus avellana*, 6m/20ft), field maple (*Acer campestre*, 6–9m/20–30ft), silver birch (*Betula pendula*, 25m/80ft) and holly (*Ilex aquifolium*, 25m/80ft but usually less) with hawthorn (*Crataegus monogyna*, 5m/16ft) at the edges of the planting (because it's smaller and would need light). Alders, in particular *Alnus glutinosa* (to 20m/65ft) are excellent trees, tolerant of most situations, particularly wet ground. Not only would the bungalow soon be hidden, but she would also be creating a wildlife haven.

A good gardener I know has a 'great neighbour', but he's such a control freak that he insists that the concrete party wall is completely bare on his side. He refers to her collection of beautiful and unusual clematis as 'your creepers' and absolutely detests her ivies. If so much as

Bupleurum fruticosum is a nice neighbourly evergreen growing on our party wall. Here it is accompanied by *Helianthus* 'Capenoch Star'.

a leaf shows over the boundary line it must be removed that day. Even when it comes to public roads, some house owners (they're invariably male) try to protect their property with elaborate arrangements of traffic cones and wheelie bins in front of their houses to prevent drivers parking – which they have every right to do – and if that doesn't work rush out and loudly harangue them. They have the same slightly mad look in their eye as the Irish sheepdogs that lie in wait for a car to go by, ever hopeful of catching one, and then dash out, barking furiously.

The worst dispute between neighbours I know of happened in Dublin and concerned a rose bed in a front garden, the owner of which had answered an ad for professional rose pruning. The landscaper involved, having agreed a price and time for the job, found that so much business was generated by the ad that he farmed some out to a young lad who arrived by bus, got muddled about directions and promptly set to in the first garden he saw, pruning roses plus everything else in sight and making all the bits into a great pile of rubbish, which he expected the boss to collect. Not only was this the wrong garden, but it was also next door to the garden where he was meant to be working. As you can imagine, the repercussions were noisy.

On the subject of noise, *Euonymus japonicus* (6m/20ft) is an ordinary-looking evergreen shrub with cheerful bright green leaves which nobody ever remarks on. Our specimen is probably as old as the house (1830), and is now 4m/12ft tall and 3m/10ft thick. Growing just outside the back door on the garden boundary, this shrub performs one of the most useful of all gardening jobs: the dense evergreen foliage is a superb noise absorber. Opposite the front door in the plantation (a narrow strip of woodland between our row of houses and the busy main road) is a mature horse chestnut (*Aesculus hippocastanum*, 25m/80ft). Even with my eyes shut I could tell you the exact day this comes into leaf in spring, when suddenly the traffic noise is muffled. The day the leaves fall in autumn the traffic is more noticeable. Something else to think about when choosing plants for your boundary: what about noise pollution?

Tulips

I never get tired of tulips, even the plain mid-pink ones, sold in bunches on street corners, tightly in bud. They look so stiff you'd think they were made of plastic, but after a few days in a warm room the stems bend in a voluptuous fashion and the petals begin to slouch about, exposing beautiful middles, often washed light blue in the centre.

Mind you, our tulips get badly treated. This year I've got seven obsolete dustbins (a few years ago there was only one), all painted lavender grey and each crammed with six to eight layers of tulips. With fifty to eighty bulbs per bin, battery hens have got nothing on my tulips, and the bulbs have to squeeze their bottoms into very small spaces. What I hope is going to be a mad and glorious mixture of colours and shapes, from the elegance of lily-flowered tulips to the frilly confections of parrot tulips, feathered and streaked Rembrandts and my favourite late double 'Carnaval de Nice' (white striped burgundy), should give a really good lasting show for six weeks.

If you're using lots of different colours together, I think it's better not to include very dark tulips, such as 'Queen of Night', as they look like a black hole in the mix and don't show up from the distance; whereas a tulip such as 'Daydream', which matures from bright yellow to luminous orange, is wonderful for lighting up bare spring soil.

On this thin, well-drained soil tulips are rarely much good after the first year. So I treat them as annuals (I discard the bulbs and chop the green tops for the compost heap) and their sparkling contribution of big flowers and bright colours compensates for my extravagance. (In other parts of the country they last well from year to year; some say that deep planting helps.) Here I plant them in waves and ribbons at the edges of the main borders beside the central canal. An intense mass of colour is what's wanted – small groups of bulbs dotted around won't have enough impact.

We don't plant until the borders are completely tidy, in late November and December, and planting takes at least two (fine) days, working flat out. Sometimes I plant forget-me-nots on top, thus presenting a lovely, well-worn gardening cliché: tulips arising out of a froth of blue. By using tulips as annuals, and throwing them away after flowering, you should avoid tulip fire disease, which is encouraged by growing tulips in the same place for too long. I've just discovered that the Dutch,

We wait until late November and early December before planting tulips.

too, also use tulips as annuals (which stops me feeling guilty). Also, the reason all the blooms in the bulb fields are picked off before they fade is that tulip fire can spread via fallen petals.

When buying tulips, concentrate on getting a good balance between early-, mid-season- and late-flowering tulips. I'm especially keen on planting lots of May-blooming cultivars, to carry the colour on through. My list will change again next year, but at the moment I always include 'Angélique', 'Apricot Beauty', 'Carnaval de Nice', 'Daydream', 'Douglas Bader', 'Elegant Lady', 'Gavota', 'Maytime', 'Peach Blossom', 'Prinses Irene', 'Pink Impression', 'Spring Green' and 'Shirley'.

Some tulips are soundly perennial here, such as the Turkish *T. sprengeri* (25cm/10in), of which I'm very fond. Shining bright red flowers appear in late May on this neat, self-seeding small tulip. However, the lady tulip (*T. clusiana*, 30cm/12in), a lovely little thing with flowers in rose pink and white, is never much good at flowering again in this garden, despite a position in full sun. On the other hand, *T.* Batalanii Group 'Bronze Charm' bloomed for twenty springs on the raised bed, until it disappeared during a big soil-changing operation.

You can see why tulips have been so admired for centuries – the flowers are beautiful even in decrepitude, when the slightest movement of air sends the petals fluttering down.

The May gap

Sun shining through beech trees, glossy young grass, leaves radiant with health – I always forget how beautiful May is from one year to the next. With high summer just around the corner, I remind myself of all there is to look forward to – roses, delphiniums, poppies and peonies. Unless of course you live on acid soil, in rhododendron and azalea country, May isn't about great sweeps of colour but more about the beauty of individual flowers.

Look at a single flower of the scrumptious pink *Paeonia suffruticosa* (1.5m/5ft), the tree peony occasionally found in old Irish gardens. This is the same floppy-petalled rose pink flower that is illustrated in the middle of *famille rose* plates, the eighteenth-century porcelain made in China for the European market. 'The most beautiful thing on earth' is how Maria Edgeworth (1767–1849), the Anglo-Irish novelist, described this tree peony. Cicely Hall, the great gardener and rescuer of old cultivars of Primrose Hill in Lucan, near Dublin, gave me a piece of her plant in the early 1980s. For many years this was the star in residence here in the small bed beside the greenhouse.

Arguments may continue about whether or not global warming is taking place, but as far as my peony is concerned the climate is changing fast. May used to be the peak of the flowering season, but recently buds have been attempting to unfold in January – worryingly early, as peonies need a proper, cold winter. So this autumn, Mary (our gardener) and I decided that the plant was looking so iffy, with such yellowing leaves, that our only recourse was to move it to a cooler position. I don't know if you've ever dug up a peony (both herbaceous and tree peonies loathe disturbance), but it can be an upsetting experience, as many roots get broken during the operation. They're so plump and flesh-like that it's a reminder that you're dealing with something very much alive. But there comes a stage in gardening where things can't go on deteriorating and action must be taken, do or die. (*Paeonia suffruticosa* is looking better now in cool part shade.)

This summer, we finally dug up the legendary tree peony *Paeonia rockii* (there is some confusion about this name; formerly 'Joseph Rock', 1.5–2m/5–7ft). I once investigated the roots of a herbaceous peony, to discover them nearly eaten away by a gang of voracious larvae of the swift moth. I sent one of the grubs off to Wisley for identification and got a letter back saying: 'Swift

moths are usually found in very weedy gardens.' When *P. rockii* began to fail, I could hardly pass by without imagining a Hogarthian underground scene. Nothing could rid my mind of what might be happening below ground. On digging up the peony, we discovered no grubs (presumably in summer they're flying around as moths, busily laying eggs) but the roots were holed and pitted, scraped and stunted – the telltale signs of a former city of baby swift moths, all stuffing their faces at the expense of my lovely plant.

However, Caucasian *Paeonia mlokosewitschii* (60cm/24in) after half a century still produces its fleeting, exquisite pale yellow bowls of flower with gilded anthers every May. My theory as to its survival is that passing swift moths, their minds occupied by egg laying (what little there is of their minds – apparently they're rather thick, primitive moths), become diverted by the metal trellis beside which my peony grows. They veer off course and lay eggs elsewhere. Good.

The giant Chatham Island forget-me-not (*Myosotidium hortensia*, 45cm/18in) is one of the thrilling plants of May. A member of the borage family, at first sight it looks like a bergenia or hosta with brilliant blue flowers; unfortunately the camera never does the colour justice. Apparently a rare plant in its native Chatham Islands, where it is threatened by wild pigs and sheep, it survives on boulder beaches accompanied by washed-up seaweed (hence the idea that a mulch of seaweed is desirable). Here it likes cool shade, on a peaty bed under a north-facing wall. We cover it with a glass cloche in winter (allowing lots of air at the sides). I reckon people didn't realize until recently how easy it is from seed, but it is now widely available. Incidentally, when the clusters of seedheads are ripening around June, they lie about on the soil surface looking dead, hanging on by a thread to the parent plant. Don't pull them off by mistake in an effort to tidy them up. I've grown this giant forget-me-not for many years and never bothered about the seaweed mulch, but remember that the enormously handsome, deeply veined, shining leaves are at precisely the right angle for slugs to practise their morning glissades.

In the week of May when the garden's most bereft of flower colour, just on the cusp between spring and summer, all is recompensed by the sparkling freshness of the various shades of green – it's as if there is a hush in the audience before the show begins. This is always the week that the camassias bloom. I particularly like the way the colour of *C. leichtlinii* subsp. *suksdorfii* 'Electra' (60cm/24in) flashes from blue to almost turquoise. The only thing you must do with these easy, long-lived bulbs for a sunny position, native to western North America, is to mark the position well so as not to plant something else on top; and remember not to say the name out loud in strange places – people might think you were saying rude things in a foreign language.

Splendour and opulence arrive in early summer when Oriental poppies (*Papaver orientale*, 90cm/3ft), with a triumphant wave to the humble smaller flowers of spring, present their lavish blooms. Go out in early morning as the

Papaver orientale 'Karine' is an excellent, medium-sized poppy.

Alstroemerias, *Iris* 'Corrida' (a present from Graham Stuart Thomas) and *Centranthus ruber* 'Albus' flowering in the garden in May

flowers unfurl their crinkled petals, and cruising bumblebees will buzz you out of the way in their rush to dive into the middle of the flower, where they will ease their way drunkenly about among the stamens, with a wave of a filigree leg in the air. An old love used to be 'Patty's Plum', a wonderful blackcurranty colour when it first opens, which dies to an ugly shade of grubby handkerchief. Popular here are self-descriptive 'Black and White' and pale salmon 'Karine'. Oriental poppies look hideous as the leaves die off after flowering; these are one of the few herbaceous perennials that you are allowed to chop back in midsummer to remove the mess.

An early summer, old-fashioned cottage garden flower is the sweet william (*Dianthus barbatus*, 45cm/18in) usually grown as a biennial. I sow it from seed in about June, prick out the seedlings into trays and then plant them out to fatten up, anywhere free of plants I can find; then I move them to permanent positions in autumn. Columbines (*Aquilegia vulgaris*, 30–60cm/1–2ft) are essential for May colour; you need to buy fresh plants or new seed from a good, large-flowered, long-spurred strain; otherwise after some years all you'll have will be washy pink, purple or medium blue self-sown seedlings.

Silver leaves

Leaves appear silver or grey for a particular reason. To protect the surfaces of the leaves from stress – from sun, drought or freezing winds – they are covered with thousands of tiny hairs, which create a silver haze, catching the sun and reflecting the light. The addition of silver foliage to a planting mix has a magical and immediate effect, and even the common summer bedding plant *Senecio cinerarea* (60cm/24in) will perk up a plant grouping straight away. This has overwintered here for many years and we cut it back hard in spring.

Convolvulus or bindweed, as you know, is an atrocious colonizer. But a close relation is one of the prettiest shrubs I grow, *Convolvulus cneorum* (50cm/20in), with narrow silky leaves and white trumpet flowers tinged with pink. A rich, moist soil rapidly causes this to grow lush and succumb to winter wet. Mine grows in dry, starving soil against a warm wall. Trim after flowering; good in a pot; propagate by cuttings. Incidentally, cuttings of grey- and silver-leaved plants don't like humid conditions, such as in a frame or under polythene. I root cuttings of plants such as lavender or pinks in an uncovered sand bed in the alpine house.

Senecio viravira (1.5m/5ft against a wall) comes from Patagonia, where the wind never seems to stop, and how this exceptionally brittle shrub survives I don't know – if you so much as look at it a bit falls off. Under the overhang of a house or tree will do nicely, provided there's plenty of sun, because the drier the position, the more brilliantly white the delicately cut leaves will be. Doesn't need pruning; does need deadheading; easy from cuttings.

In case you're weary of my constant mentions of 'sun and good drainage', I saw *Astelia nervosa* (90cm/3ft) growing wild in the shade of nothofagus or southern beech trees in New Zealand, in areas of high rainfall. It's been growing here in a shady north-facing peaty bed for twenty-five years, just sitting there, with its long, slender, metallic leaves, like a great silver multi-legged spider. I've only ever divided it once. Occasionally I tidy it up by cutting the old leaves away (you can't say that's heavy-duty maintenance).

Astelia chathamica (90cm/3ft) is a spectacular and very easily grown plant, with much wider leaves, like shimmering silver phormium. In colder areas this would be my top choice as a container plant.

Propagate by division, from which it's slow to recover, or fresh seed. Protect from slugs; otherwise they will munch up the outer hairs and make green patches on the beautiful leaves. It's encouraging to see *Astelia* spp. listed under 'Plants for dry shady areas' in *The Gardener's Encyclopaedia of New Zealand Native Plants* by Yvonne Cave and Valda Paddison (Random House New Zealand, 1999).

Celmisia semicordata (30cm/12in), one of the New Zealand daisies, looks like a small astelia, with evergreen lustrous silver leaves and large white daisies on white felt stems in May. This is neither common nor easy to grow. Essentials are full exposure and sun, to remind it of the high light intensity it has in the wild, where it grows in high rainfall alpine regions (up to 160cm/300in of rain a year) on South Island, such as Mount Cook. Good drainage, plenty of moisture in the growing season and cool damp Irish weather are what's wanted, as heat and humidity spell death (they also do well in Northumberland and Scotland).

Thrilled by possession of one of these super daisies, gardeners are inclined to position it (as they would any other silver plant) in a sheltered corner protected by a shrub. Then they begin worrying about winter wet. They won't need to worry for long: the celmisia will shortly disappear, as celmisias cannot stand being overshadowed by neighbouring plants and detest drying out. My celmisias are planted on the raised bed, within easy reach of the water barrel in times of drought. New Zealand plants are not accustomed to rich soil, so we mixed a lot of peat into the area. Propagate by division in September. Many sections will come away without roots – simply insert the pieces very firmly up to the base of the rosette and roots should form by spring. Deadheading required; tidy up the plants in autumn by removing dead leaves with a sharp downward tug.

Senecio candidans was given to me in the 1980s with this name by Molly Sanderson, the renowned Northern Irish gardener. It comes from the Falkland Islands and southern Patagonia. Years later I saw it huddled on a wind-blasted stony Patagonian beach, within sight of nesting penguins. The next batch of seeds came from Jonathan Shackleton's recent trip to Antarctica via the Falkland Islands. Despite the measly yellow flowers, the leaves are glistening large ovals of dreamy silver grey. Division is possible, as are cuttings and seed, but this is by no means an easy plant. If slugs could fly, their ultimate holiday destination would be the beaches of southern Patagonia, or my raised bed, where my most recent specimen is still, for the moment, surviving.

Verbascum 'Frosted Gold' (60cm/24in) came in the 1970s from Mrs Desmond Underwood, who had a good nursery in Essex, specializing in grey and silver plants. Rarely seen, this is a neat, totally perennial verbascum, with a long display of lemon-yellow flowers and large pale silver leaves. Being sterile, it does not produce seed, so you have to propagate it, very slowly, from cuttings. It looks good year round, except for July, when it needs deadheading and tidying.

ABOVE *Celmisia semicordata* 'David Shackleton'
BELOW *Senecio candidans*

Has it got a little brother?

Of course I'd never have a polythene bag in my handbag – I'd never dream of being so presumptuous. However, there often seems to be one in my pocket – heaven knows how it got there – just at the right time: when I'm standing in somebody else's garden, in earnest discussion with the owner, in front of a desirable plant. The next step is delicate. How to put the idea of giving me a cutting into the garden owner's head, so that it seems as if it was their idea in the first place?

Lady Moore, one of the greats of early-twentieth-century Irish gardening, would remark, 'Has it got a little brother?' So charmingly put, so hard to refuse.

'Is it easy from cuttings?' neatly entraps the garden owner into boasting how easy the cuttings are to root, so they have to give you a bit immediately. The only way they can wriggle out is with the swift reply 'Wrong time of year.' At which point you come in with the big guns of 'Where did you get it?'

Years ago, in Ireland, high garden society only liked to spread special plants to their friends and equals. 'Uncle Clarence brought it back from China in the 1890s,' they'd say, pressing a small pot into your hands after a garden lunch, with the understanding that this was not for general distribution. In fact it came back to me that a prominent figure of the Irish gardening world, on handing a rare plant to a favoured guest, remarked 'Don't give it to Helen – she'll only give it away.'

Rare plants were almost to be dealt in, like a currency. With one went the same playground sound 'Na na na na na' that we sometimes hear floating over from the school at the back of the garden, the triumphant cry of 'I've got it, you haven't.' But the wonderful thing now, with the advent of the excellent *RHS Plant Finder*, is that that particular sort of snobbish one-upmanship has gone down the drain. You can order anything you want, in the middle of the night if you feel like it, via the Internet. The whole show-off aspect of gardening has had the rug pulled from underneath it. You don't have to persuade anybody to give you anything; all you need is the proper Latin name and a Visa card.

Taking cuttings in somebody else's garden is stealing, however creative the method. A friend mentioned that she had an unusually light-fingered aunt who instructed her niece to take cuttings always from the back of the bed, rather than the front. Pinching cuttings is taboo now, but we must remember that in the garden culture of the mid-twentieth century it was considered perfectly correct to take cuttings – people were only 'rescuing' plants. The same friend told me the satisfying story of how she noticed a wilting primula towards the end of her garden. On digging it up, she found the soil and roots heaving in vine weevil, but as a visiting group were on the way she decided to leave it there until they'd gone. After their departure she returned to discover that the plant – weevils and all – had disappeared.

Little brother

If there was ever any justification for taking cuttings it would be in a neglected garden beside a ruined house, where the great survivors bloom on, such as the wonderful common peony *Paeonia officinalis* 'Rubra Plena' (60cm/24in), grown in gardens since the sixteenth century, unnamed roses that may have disappeared from cultivation (in which case it's your duty to propagate and distribute them) or perhaps an unusual daffodil.

When visitors are here I get edgy when people start fingering plants. You never know what's on their mind – an innocent daydream, or something more sinister. Sometimes I can see that somebody is so longing for a plant that I want to give it them anyway. Occasionally I read their eyes and see something different: their day out includes a plant or two – of mine, that is.

Going green

I was brought up in a cloud of chemicals. Anything that wriggled, slithered, fluttered or crawled was dispatched by the appropriate toxic preparation. More than four legs were suspect; no legs at all could be worse. If it wasn't malathion, it was DDT. The answer to all our problems was to be found in an atomizer, bottle, sachet or can. Terrorists of the insect, rodent or spider variety were to be treated with zero tolerance. Nature's impeccably created order – such as what creature ate which and was then, in turn, eaten – was turned on its head.

It was the custom of the day, and of course I went along with it. The killing shelf of the potting shed was tightly packed with containers. In the late 1970s, in order to deal with an infestation of vine weevils, local garden experts advised me to drench the whole garden, square yard after square yard, with a solution of dieldrin. The operation took three weeks. I'm told that dieldrin (related to aldrin) is now considered fifty-five times more dangerous than DDT. Vine weevil larvae seem to be covered with some kind of waxy coat and even a fortnight's soak in a solution of Jeyes fluid (the old-fashioned cure-all with a strong smell of hospital) had no effect whatsoever. Dieldrin did the trick, but what else did it kill at the same time? Deep guilt set in.

There were no vine weevils for about fifteen years but sometime in the mid-1990s I was extraordinarily pleased when I found one of the telltale white grubs underneath one of their favourite foods, a primrose. At last a sign of the soil's recovery and a slight lessening of guilt.

To be honest I didn't really believe that if you leave pests alone, the balance will adjust and you'll never get a build-up of one kind in particular. But not only did this prove a reality: it happened remarkably quickly. We haven't sprayed the roses against greenfly for three years now, and the sucking hordes of aphids that used to arrive in May have visibly shrunk. We ordered pest-busting ladybird larvae. When they arrived by post, we could barely find a greenfly to introduce them to for some supper – I suppose they'd been gobbled up by young blue tits or hoverflies.

There's nothing more satisfying than the squelching sound of a cluster of greenfly being squeezed between finger and thumb. Certainly quick and definitely organic. I do it automatically, while talking to visitors and/or thinking about something else.

Of all the known creepy-crawlies, spiders used to be my greatest problem. Just to imagine how their thistledown legs would feel scuttering around on my skin was appalling. When I lived in London, large ones would invade my flat, especially in autumn. I used to ring the police when particularly big ones turned up – I couldn't possibly stay in the building, let alone the same room, as a big spider. (Those were the days when all policemen were older and bigger than me.) I remember explaining to a constable on the doorstep about the immensity of the problem, and being pleased when he agreed that yes, it was indeed a whopper of a spider. It was only when I read that any spider you met on its own was just a lonely creature looking for a friend that I started feeling better about them.

I often think how lucky we are to live in a late Regency Dublin house. Elegance personified – but only at first sight. However, it's not only Val, I and the two dogs who live here: there are almost certainly several (never believe there's only one) of what a friend

To encourage ladybirds, stop spraying with insecticide.

describes as having 'long tails and naked ankles'. The rodents I catch a glimpse of occasionally in the yard have glossy coats and are probably looking after large families nesting in the bottom of the compost heap. Mr Reginald (an aggressive small wire-haired dachsund) has managed to dispatch two, with the flourish of a celebrity bullfighter, tossing them up in the air and splashing blood all over the terrace – surely a fairer death, in so far as there is such a thing, than the slow agony of the blue-pelleted rat poison.

Veg in raised beds

The main reason for growing your own is all to do with greed and the incomparable taste of vegetables that have incurred no air miles and are served with an invisible sauce, for which the only ingredient is loving care from seed packet to table, plus a sprinkling of gardener's pride.

Take carrots. From the school carrot, trying to hide in glutinous brown gravy, to the elegantly prepared restaurant matchstick, to me they all have a sour aftertaste. The most deceptive are the baby carrots, all lined up in their plastic bag, like the appendages of cherubim and seraphim, suggestive of sweetness and youth, decorated with fresh green topknots. I don't know what these are fed on, but to me they taste of diluted pig manure. (Yes, I do know what this tastes like – remember that smell and taste are very close.) Even their luminous orange colour looks suspiciously like the predominantly chemical drink formerly known as orangeade.

The other thing that concerns me about vegetables – a thought that occupies my mind whenever I'm contemplating the veg stands in the supermarket – is could it be that vegetables and fruit now die from the inside? You'd expect a peach or apple to be bruised or nibbled on the outside, but sometimes, when you've bought one and eaten as far as the middle, you notice a pale brown, seeping rot. Scary.

Back to carrots: a home-grown carrot, just pulled from the earth, is sweet, tender and crunchy all at once. Not easy to grow in Dublin, because of carrot fly. My most successful experiment with carrots was when I grew them in dustbins. I read somewhere that this carrot pest is aeronautically challenged and cannot fly more than 60cm/12in high. It flutters along, presumably thinking, in so far as carrot flies think, 'Hmm . . . do I smell carrot?' and then it's splat as they collide with the side of the dustbin. And it's bye-bye fly and hello carrot. All very satisfactory. To be doubly sure, you can cover the top of the dustbin with some horticultural fleece or fine netting, and tie it on with a bit of string, so that it looks like a giant old-fashioned jam pot and cover.

For beginners the easiest veg of all (my cousin Joanna recommended this to me when I started growing veg) is Swiss chard. This looks like spinach, and is sometimes sold as such, but it has a pronounced succulent white midrib and is closely related to beetroot. Succulent, leafy and green, this grew so well that we ate it every day for about ten days and then suddenly couldn't face it again for a month. All it requires is fertile soil and sun. (A vegetable plot absolutely must have sun – vegetables only eke their lives away in shade.) The good thing about Swiss chard is that you can go on picking it for months and have another crop of seedlings coming on elsewhere to follow on. When you get tired of eating it boiled, lightly cook it, stir in chopped onion softened in butter and smother in a good cheese sauce. Any vehicle for butter and cheese sauce is worth investigating.

The second essential vegetable worth growing at home is purple sprouting broccoli. Rapidly being overtaken by the tough, mostly imported, long-lasting bright green stuff, purple sprouting is a delicate creature that wilts the moment it's picked. It needs steaming for a few minutes and deserves lavish amounts of melted butter. Sow in June, ideally in a row in spare ground outdoors, but as I never have the necessary spare ground I sow it in a pot and prick out the seedlings individually into 15cm/6in pots. The young plants should be in their permanent position, 60–90cm/2–3ft apart, by August. All members of the cabbage family should be very firmly planted; also, it's quite OK, indeed desirable, as it prevents wind rock, to insert the plants more deeply than they were originally.

Your next problem will be the local pigeons. We have an exceptionally stupid pigeon in this garden, known for obvious reasons as Daffodil, as he repeatedly falls in love with his own reflection in the canal and tumbles in (he always struggles out again, as the water's only 15cm/6in deep), but you need only one brainy pigeon to work out how to get at the broccoli. I take no chances and cover the crop with netting the moment it's planted. Incidentally, I've always had a theory that a veg tastes particularly good served along with something that eats it – pigeon with broccoli, rabbit with lettuce, bacon and cabbage, goat with just about anything leafy, and so on.

Arguments continue between those who prefer climbing French beans to the old-fashioned scarlet runner. Whatever your opinion, don't let a summer go by without one of them at least. A wigwam of beans looks good anywhere in the garden. You need only 90cm/3ft square of decent soil in sun and total commitment to watering. A mistake often made by beginners is to plant out tender vegetables (such as beans, courgettes and tomatoes) too soon. Young plants are slow to recover from cold, wet May weather. Much hardier are broad beans, which I absolutely adore. We usually sow these in mid-November. I even like the older beans, but only if they are individually peeled after cooking and reheated with olive oil and parsley, thus providing a deliciously starchy green sludge.

My raised beds for veg (I've built no fewer than four different veg gardens in the last ten years) are usually about 3.5m/12ft long and 1.5m/5ft wide. I've also found beds 90cm/3ft square useful for many things, such as wigwams for beans and peas, salad crops, Swiss chard, dwarf beans, courgettes and herbs. The paths between them have been raked earth or gravel. I remember the

Digging manure into a raised bed for veg

kitchen garden at home in Scotland, where the rich Perthshire soil certainly grew wonderful veg, but as everything was planted in long rows with no permanent paths, an expedition there invariably involved wellington boots, with which there was always the spider problem – that is, that there might be one hiding in the toe of the boot and I wouldn't be able to get the boot off fast enough before fainting.

Not wishing to bang on too long about it, here is the manifesto of the raised bed: you can reach all parts of the bed without treading on it; when it comes to rotation of crops it's easy to remember what went where the previous year; as there is a greater depth of richly prepared topsoil available to the plants you can plant at greater density than you can in rows; you can dash out in pouring rain to pick something without spreading mud everywhere; the wellington boot problem is overcome; any soil preparation such as digging isn't too daunting, as it's in small portions; and from an aesthetic point of view, a nicely laid-out formal pattern of small beds is always pleasing. By the way, the idea of edging the beds in box is all very pretty, but not a good one if you're serious about growing veg, as box needs regular attention with the shears, harbours slugs and encroaches on available nutrients and moisture. Instead, if you want your veg garden to be decorative, scatter seeds of pot marigolds (*Calendula officinalis*), nasturtiums and heartsease (*Viola tricolor*), sow crimson-flowered broad beans and view it all through a haze of fennel.

The two things I regret not doing the moment we moved here are (a) planting a yew hedge and (b) installing an asparagus bed. We turned down both ideas on account of how slow they'd be. But I have grown (in a nearby allotment, now sadly gone) the most delicious vegetable in the world, seakale, the aristocrat of the cabbage family, which most people have never eaten and have only heard about as they've seen, in smart garden shops, fancy expensive reproduction terracotta seakale pots. All you need is a large black plastic bucket, as used by builders, to put over the seakale shoots in winter and keep out every chink of light as the plants develop into deliciously succulent blanched leaves, which you boil for fifteen minutes and cover in melted butter. Long lived, easily propagated from root cuttings, decorative in the garden – what more do you want?

Burglar-proof plants

I once wrote a piece, somewhat tongue in cheek, about how to keep the neighbours out by planting *Rosa filipes* 'Kiftsgate'. A few days after it appeared in print, I had a man on the telephone. His neighbours, apparently, were no laughing matter. Could I guarantee that if he planted 'Kiftsgate' his neighbour problem would finally be fixed? I could see that the conversation was heading rapidly towards litigation if my glib suggestion didn't work. I muttered about large dogs as back-up for the rose and tried to steer the conversation gracefully away.

Rose 'Kiftsgate' has tremendous lure for a beginner. It was discovered in Kiftsgate, the romantic Cotswold garden, and named in the 1950s by Graham Stuart Thomas. Now apparently the specimen there is the biggest rose in England, and when last measured it was 25 x 28 x 15m/80 x 90 x 50ft high, deep and wide. Young growths on a plant extend to 6m/20ft in a year. No trouble, I thought: I'll just chop off surplus ones. But the thorns are something else. It has backwards-pointing sharp hooks that are specially designed for clinging on to anything near by and hoisting themselves up to the treetops. One can rapidly go off a rose when the branches whip round and attach themselves in several places to the skin on the underside of your arms, so that if you try to extract one, the others jab their way further in.

I decided I couldn't cope with such a rambunctious rose, and I also had to take out the old Irish rambling rose 'Belvedere', which was nearly smothering a huge old pear and taking much of the light from a long herbaceous border. But 'Paul's Himalayan Musk' still tumbles over the wall from next door, festooned with pale pink blossom, the prettiest thing in the garden for two weeks of the year. It too is vigorous, but its thorns aren't quite so vicious. We prune away the stems that have flowered in late summer (the ones we can reach, that is).

If, in order to heave himself over the wall, a burglar grabbed a handful of stems of the fuchsia-flowered gooseberry (*Ribes speciosum*, 4m/12ft), you'd hear furious squawks from the other end of Dublin. This Californian shrub looks very like a fuchsia, blooms very early in the year, in February, isn't remotely fussy, has nice shiny bright green leaves that are summer dormant in drought and in the wild is pollinated by hummingbirds. The prickles, not easily seen at first, are full of spite and

No sensible burglar would care to confront the vigorous rose 'Paul's Himalayan Musk', which tumbles over our wall from next door.

horribly sharp. Still, this is an easy, long-suffering shrub that's grown and flowered here for many years – a good choice for a shady garden in the more challenging parts of town.

I suppose the most fiendish spikes of all belong to the Chilean bromeliad *Puya alpestris* (1.2m/4ft). I was weeding near it one day, feeling as ratty and unsettled as usual, when I had what could only be called an epiphany: suddenly I noticed the puya was in bloom. I couldn't believe the colour: the flowers had the same iridescence and greenish turquoise as the middle of a peacock's feather, forming a great 1.5m/5ft spire of metallic shining blossom. The flowers didn't last long, and the plant has since died, but for that particular moment the sun shone on the garden as never before. By the way, I picked up an excellent way of growing puyas from a visit to Roger Raiche's garden in California: large terracotta drainpipes standing on end were forming extra well-drained containers. A puya we grew that way here (I'm not certain which species) produced beautiful greenish yellow flowers only the second year after planting. A group of three or five upended drainpipes, all planted with succulents or bromeliads, looks terrific.

With regard to burglars (one shouldn't be sexist about this: just because children's comics always show male burglars in striped jerseys doesn't mean to say female burglars aren't as common), I hope that next time he or she visits the one who stole my gnome loses his or her trousers on the way over the garden wall and tumbles bottom first into the berberis and gets stuck, and that the burglar who stole the silver the only time we got it out of the bank for a party makes a grab for *Rosa sericea* subsp. *omeiensis* f. *pteracantha*, a mega-prickly rose, and then slips into something loose in Daisy's favourite lavatory spot.

Cuttings

My main reason for taking cuttings – and this applies to most women who went to school in the 1950s – is that I'm haunted by guilt. Every time the headmistress (Miss Dodds, she was – I don't think any of us knew her Christian name) swept into the school chapel, her long black gown swaying to the rhythm of her stride (I always suspected her of giving her gown an extra twirl), an all-pervading feeling of guilt would descend. Once down, it remained for the day, and as there were few days that didn't include at least one visit to the chapel, I spent several years under a grey pall.

If I'm not careful, guilt steps into the garden and sits on my shoulder, just out of eyeshot, like a resentful black bird, nagging away to himself. He doesn't approve of my digging plants up, oh no – what am I doing to that perfectly good plant? How dare I hack into that living thing? But if I can quickly propagate a plant before taking it out and have a rooted cutting ready to move elsewhere or give away, that wretched bird is silenced, as if I had put a dark cloth over his head, just as we used to put a black cover over the budgerigar's cage at night.

TAKING THE CUTTINGS

Choose a time when you're unlikely to be disturbed for half an hour. Collect sharp secateurs and a polythene bag. Most cuttings should be 8–10cm/3–4in long and although many cuttings can be taken with a little heel of older wood (by using a little downward tug), if the cutting would end up too long if taken with a heel, use the secateurs to make a clean cut just below a leaf joint. I think the advantage of a heel is that the stem is firmer and less sappy at that point. The shoot is better supported and less likely to collapse. Put the cuttings into the bag as you go.

TO PREPARE THE CUTTING

Cleanly nip off some of the lower leaves. If the heel has a long tail on it, level it off neatly. The reason for taking the lower leaves and the end of the heel off is that you don't want to encourage rot of any sort.

CUTTING MIX

For my cutting mix, until a good, fast draining substitute for peat is found, I'm continuing to use a mix of equal parts of moist peat mixed with clean sand (if necessary, rinse the sand several times through an old kitchen sieve and leave to dry off). Sometimes I use a mix of vermiculite and peat. (Potting compost is considered too rich for cuttings.)

Choose a small pot, 7cm/3in for a single cutting, or 10cm/4in for three to five cuttings. At busy times of year, such as spring and early autumn, I keep a bucket of mix handy, so that cuttings don't have to wait while I prepare some. The only cuttings that can with advantage be left around for a day are pelargoniums and some succulents; the end of the cuttings dries off and forms a callus, an important first stage of the rooting process. I never bother with rooting powder. To me it's like putting a bit of green crystallized angelica on top of an iced cake. So what? It's optional.

PUTTING IN THE CUTTINGS

The hole for the cutting, made by sticking your finger into the mix, should be at the edge of the pot. This is where the drainage is better. If you've got more than one cutting in the pot, make sure you have an uneven number of cuttings, three, five or seven, or, as a great Irish gardener used to say, 'The fairies will get them.' Beginners often make the mistake of not firming the cuttings properly and also not ensuring that the bases of the cuttings are in perfect contact with the bottom of the hole. Water once, using a can with a fine spray, firm gently again and give another sprinkle.

WHAT TO DO WITH THE CUTTINGS

Cuttings have no roots. Their leaves lose moisture from the moment they're cut off the parent plant. What you do now depends on what facilities you have. Either use a heated propagator (I've never had one); or you could place the pot of cuttings under a bell jar in the greenhouse or in a shaded cold frame, where plants should root. If the weather's still warm you could put the pot in a polythene bag, support the bag by tying the top firmly to a cane and place it in a shaded corner.

LATE-SUMMER CUTTINGS

These are the cuttings I take most of. In fact I take these from late summer through autumn, but the ones taken early are much quicker to root. These are stem cuttings, ideally about 10cm/4in long, taken with a heel. I do this with plants I need more of, plus tender plants that might be lost in winter outdoors.

Reminder of some plants suitable for late-summer cuttings: abutilon, amicia, felicia, fuchsia, hebe, hedera, *Helichrysum petiolare*, hydrangea, lavatera, lavandula, osteospermum, pelargonium, penstemon, phygelius, malva, rosmarinus, many salvias, santolina, senecio, sparmannia, verbena.

BASAL CUTTINGS

Certain herbaceous plants can be increased by taking short basal or tip cuttings of soft young spring growth. This works well with lythrum, *Gentiana asclepiadea*, nepeta, sedum and delphinium, for example. A senior member of the Delphinium Society told me that you should take short basal cuttings of delphiniums as soon as the shoots are 10cm/4in high, probably in March. Insert the cuttings in a small pot of neat perlite, stand the pot in a saucer of water which you keep replenished and place it in a greenhouse. This works.

ROOT CUTTINGS

This is a satisfying method of propagation because it usually works, although it takes some time, with eryngiums, echinops, limonium and crambe, for example. In early winter, scrape away the soil or dig carefully round the plant to expose the roots. Cut off bits of thickish root, making a straight cut at the top and a sloping cut at the bottom. It's important to insert the pieces of root the right way up, and to cover the top with only 7mm/¼in or so of cutting mix. Lay thinner roots, such as those of phlox and chamerion, horizontally. Put the pots under glass or in a cold frame for winter.

Glass bell jars are expensive but you sometimes see plastic ones, which are just as good. I now stand each pot of cuttings on a large upturned pot saucer, which is standing in an even bigger pot saucer full of water. So far no slugs have tried swimming the channel between the two.

LEAF CUTTINGS

A useful method for rooting any of the *Gesneriaceae* family, which includes African violets. This is the way I root streptocarpus: choose a middle-sized healthy leaf with a piece of leaf stalk and stick it into the cutting mix about a third the way up the leaf. You only need 2.5cm/1in of leaf above the cutting mix, so cut the rest off. Water once, using a fine spray. Put the pot in a polythene bag (preferably a ziplock); blow into the bag to puff it up. Don't allow the leaves to touch the polythene

Cuttings rooting in sand in a well-ventilated alpine house

and thus encourage rot. Close firmly at the top and leave in the shady end of a cool north-facing room of the house for several months, after which you should notice tiny plants forming at the bottom of the leaves.

HARDWOOD CUTTINGS

I've used this method for rooting roses. In early autumn take 23–30cm/9–12in cuttings of healthy wood with a heel. Put the cuttings in a narrow trench with plenty of sharp sand at the bottom in an out-of-the-way part of the garden. Trample firmly in and don't disturb for a year. I also often root roses in summer under the bell jar in the greenhouse, taking 10cm/4in cuttings of just-flowered shoots, sometimes with a heel.

If a particular plant is tricky to root, I try it at several different times of year, especially mid- to late summer for shrubs (such as hollies, azara, itea, *Magnolia grandiflora*), choosing semi-ripe wood. The only time I ever rooted the lovely difficult-to-propagate *Berberis temolaica* (1.5m/5ft) was by taking cuttings in December.

Apart from the old-fashioned bell jar, which is in constant use in the greenhouse, my most successful method of rooting cuttings is in the small, constantly ventilated greenhouse that used to be used as an alpine house. There is a 12cm/5in deep bed of sand there, unshaded, and it is right under my nose. I make a hole with my finger in the sand, stick in the cutting, firm it in and water. I'm always going by on my way to the potting shed, so I quickly notice if the sand has dried out and the cuttings need spraying. Dianthus, named violas and silver-leaved plants, all of which dislike the humid air of enclosed conditions, do well here. A small glass-topped cold frame on a sand bed should provide similar conditions.

Division

If a plant could read my thoughts, it might feel very edgy indeed. I could be thinking about chopping it up into bits and planting a lovely big spread of it. My American friend the wonderful gardener Rob Proctor, admits he sometimes plants in drifts of one, while I (Mrs Do-what-I-say-and-not-what-I-do herself), despite my endless lecturing on the importance of mass planting, am always buying one of something and planting it as a singleton.

I often propagate a plant even before putting it into the earth – after all, I've probably spent an hour deciding, with division in mind, which was the largest specimen available in the garden centre. My reasoning is that it's better to disturb the roots before a plant goes into the ground than wait until the roots are nicely settled and then haul it out again.

No plant deserves to be carried around the garden, roots in the air, while you evaluate degrees of sun, shade and moisture and imagine exactly how it will look next to the pink phlox. Often I find that in order to place something correctly at least three other moves have to be thought out. So, before dividing anything, decide where you are going to put it. Be all ready with buckets of garden compost for enriching the soil, spade, fork, watering can, secateurs and so on.

Plants with a mass of fibrous roots (Michaelmas daisies, astilbes, heleniums, eupatoriums, galegas, for example) usually divide easily, while division doesn't work well with taprooted plants, such as eryngiums. Easily divided small plants (such as *Campanula persicifolia*) you can pull apart with your hands. With very tangled roots you can place two forks back to back in the middle of the clump and rock them backwards and forwards to encourage the clump to part, or carry the plant to a hard surface like a path and chop the roots up with a sharp spade. All rapid spreaders should be divided into quite small pieces. Rather than making lots of different planting holes and putting handfuls of garden compost in the bottom of each, it's better gardening practice to prepare a few square yards all at once, giving the soil a really good dig and stirring to aerate it. Plants should be spaced roughly 30cm/1ft apart. Water everything, even if it's raining, to settle the roots in.

Herbaceous plants rapidly use up available food in the surrounding soil, and long-established clumps often die off in the middle. I divide such plants in order to make large drifts, but also

Ranunculus constantinopolitanus 'Plenus' recovered its former gloss when divided and moved into fresh soil.

because I need an excuse to empty a small area of plants, to dig in humus for replenishment. Divide up the healthy outside of the clump and throw away the baldy centre. You may need to cut up plants with woody roots, such as tough grasses, using a saw, and you will need your best sharp kitchen knife for others. Sometimes it's better to swill the roots around in a bucket of water so you can see properly which bit has a good growing shoot, and if there's a possibility of vine weevil grubs or caterpillars of the swift moth I always wash the roots, in the hope of preventing the enemy from establishing fresh battlefields.

As for the best time for division, many herbaceous plants move well in autumn (except kniphofias, grasses, some asters, and plants tender in your area). The argument for early autumn division (of which I approve, as I'm usually itching to get on with the moves) is that the soil is still warm and the roots will be settled before winter. I don't cut back other herbaceous stuff yet, so that I can gauge height and space better. In colder climates spring division is best. Division in late autumn means that roots sit in cold soil, but some gardeners argue that cutting off green herbaceous stems early weakens the plant, and division is best left to November/December. There's a lot to be said for dividing plants when you think about it (even in midsummer in this garden), and once the idea of moving something hits me I can't wait. Especially if something is 'going back' – not looking as good as last year – I usually have it out of the ground immediately and then nurse it in a new position.

Certain plants can be left in the same position for many years, among them peonies (*Paeonia*), day lilies (*Hemerocallis*), Oriental poppies (*Papaver orientale*), veratrums, hellebores and kirengeshoma. Others, such as willow gentian (*Gentiana asclepiadea*), baptisias, dictamnus, alstroemerias and *Gillenia trifoliata*, should never be disturbed.

Five shrubs with good leaves

Aucuba or spotted laurel (*Aucuba japonica*, 2m/7ft) has spent the last few decades in the doldrums of gardening fashion (although the late, great Christopher Lloyd had great admiration for these relicts of Victorian taste). I went outside just now to inspect my thirty-year-old specimen, which defiantly thrives in inhospitable shade. If ever 'a flower is born to blush unseen,/And waste its sweetness on the desert air', this is it. I picked a sprig and had a close look. It's in flower, poor thing, with panicles of tiny, watery maroon blossoms – I'd never noticed. Rather like your fattest, plainest friend when you ask her to a party, this plant is pleased to be here, just happy to be invited. Still, it's a cracking, multi-spotted bright yellow and green leafy plant, and all our gardens have a third-class position in need of occupation. There's a very smart and desirable aucuba from the lower slopes (therefore likely to be tender) of Emei Shan (Mount Omei) in China, namely *Aucuba omeiensis*. This has the greenest, shiniest and biggest of toothed leaves. I must get it.

The velvet groundsel or California geranium (*Senecio petasitis*, but you sometimes see it listed as *Roldana petasitis*, shrubby, 2m/7ft) has leaves of a beautiful shape, lovely and soft to touch. Although it often looks winter-bashed in spring (when clusters of harsh yellow daisies appear), it makes a good recovery by summer, and one has lived here, sheltered by a wall, for the last ten years. Cuttings are easily rooted, and if the plant looks a mess at any stage, hack it back to ground level and it will rapidly renew itself. Overwintered cuttings provide good showy leaves for summer bedding.

Easy, long lived and suitable for small gardens, *Mahonia* x *wagneri* 'Moseri' (90cm/3ft) is an uncommon little mahonia with clusters of yellow flowers in spring nicely set off by leaves flushed reddish bronze. In early summer the young leaves unfold a sensational bright coral pink, immensely attractive to greenfly (I wash these off with jets of cold water and squash what's left between finger and thumb). This has been here for over thirty years and I've never ever considered removing it.

Desmodium yunnanense is a beautiful member of the pea family, for which I've a soft spot, as legumes seem tolerant of the conditions here. The young leaves of this Chinese deciduous shrub are large, oval and silver-green and remain beautiful all summer, and the flowers are purple pink.

Senecio petasitis, with a blue salvia for which I've been given many different names.

You can cut it down to within 30cm/12in of ground level, but in very mild gardens (such as Mount Stewart) it grows to 4m/12ft against a sunny wall. Officially this lesser-known plant is listed as zone 9, but I think a colder garden would be acceptable with a deep mulch.

Phormiums or New Zealand flax are actually perennial herbs but I think of them as shrubs. The gardening world is divided between those with a mild, temperate climate who can grow them and those who can't. The former are inclined to be a bit sniffy about variegated phormiums (as I am), while the latter would give half their granny to own one. In Ireland, phormiums grow rather too well, and in the south and west you can see great clusters of them on roadsides and roundabouts. The problem is that when spoilt for choice gardeners are tempted to plant the red cultivar, the purple one, the yellow and green variegated one, the multi-coloured one with salmon pink stripes, plus any other colour they can get hold of – all in the same bed. You may think I'm snotty for liking the plain green species, but whereas in summer it's quite OK to see lots of bright shades, in the low but very beautiful Irish winter light these colours are too much of a jolt. I did grow *Phormium tenax* 'Cream Delight', a hybrid of *P. colensoi* (90cm/3ft) and liked it a lot, but it was the only phormium in the garden at the time. Of course, when I began the garden here I bought every one I saw, in spite of being repeatedly told that the large species, *P. tenax* (4m/12ft), would get too big – of course I didn't believe it. Out it eventually came. The same fate overtook my crimson version of the cabbage palm (*Cordyline australis,* 12m/40ft) from New Zealand. The good news for people with unsuitable climates is that you can bring a potted phormium into the house for winter, provided the room is bright and warm with lots of windows.

Containers

Growing plants in pots is the most experimental gardening of all. What I love is the impermanence of container gardening. Bought yet another plant? Can't think where to put it? Simple: buy another pot. With containers a whole new universe is revealed. Tropical plants spend summer outside, lilies scent evenings near windows and doors, small trees in pots provide screening, hydrangeas light up dark corners and tasty herbs and salads are ready and waiting by the kitchen. You can move large pots around on trolleys or castors and try them in different places.

If you don't like last year's creation, never do it again. Take my sudden brainwave, *circa* 1996, of a tower of petunias (a pot of petunias, within a pot of more petunias, with yet another pot of petunias stuck on top). By autumn of that year I had developed a deep loathing for my flowery mauve wedding cake. A floral nightmare, totally unacceptable. What suspect taste! How could I? But still I believe, every May, that this is the year that I'll make the best containers ever.

Some potted plants stay in out-of-the-way corners until they are looking their best and then make their debut in the limelight. For example, the corkscrew hazel (*Corylus avellana* 'Contorta', 4m/12ft) is hidden away in the corner of the yard in summer, when it has very dull leaves. In autumn it swaps places with the imposing succulent *Agave americana* (90cm/3ft) and I sink it, still in its pot, within a gravel-filled larger pot in a sunny place beside the canal, so that I can admire its beautiful winter silhouette of leafless, twisty branches. In spring *A. americana*, which I have tucked away in a dry corner under polythene, comes out for the summer and the hazel is demoted to the shade.

Just about any plant you can think of can be grown in a pot, but whatever you plant in a pot will be completely dependent on you and how much time you have. For example, the large *Hydrangea serrata* 'Blue Deckle' (1.5m/5ft), which we've been growing in a pot on the terrace for the last twelve years, gets a whole can of water most days in summer. What needs to be said a thousand times (I know you've read it before) is that once peat-based potting mix has dried out, it's difficult to get it thoroughly soaked through again. That's why I prefer soil-based compost (such as John Innes) for anything other than short-term bedding plants. Automatic watering is good, but it only goes so far: the lucky plants get the lion's share and the remainder only a trickle. Make life easy for yourself by using a few really big pots rather than lots of little ones. It's easier to be a better gardener by using large pots, as plants in them are slower to dry out and roots have space to delve.

I think one of the best lessons in container gardening can be seen at Great Dixter, the late Christopher Lloyd's garden in East Sussex. Here you see imaginative selections of potted plants grouped together by the front door. By standing your pots close to each other, instead of scattering them around like currants in a Danish, you make one splendid feature. They prevent each other from drying out too fast and blowing over. You can shuffle them round, putting the glamorous ones in the middle and swapping faded plants with fresh ones as often as you want.

Apart from watering, the serious work of the year is the annual repotting and checking out of permanent plantings. Unless the pots are huge, we turn them out annually in spring, right down to the drainage at the bottom. We entirely renew the potting mix of pots that regularly have two bedding seasons. Backbreaking, yes – it's no use pretending otherwise – but by giving your containers a good overhaul you clear out all the creepy-crawlies (not to mention vine weevil larvae) that might be ensconced at the base.

I'm now growing several roses in pots, including 'Dainty Bess', 'Irene Watts' and 'Souvenir du Docteur Jamain', (a) because I still love them, but I don't think roses mix well with more contemporary plantings, and (b) because I want to get really close to the individual flowers, to sample their scent and observe how lovely they are. Even with the method (now much derided by the gardening cognoscenti) of growing roses in a bed all to themselves, you couldn't get up close and personal to the actual blooms, which is the whole point of growing them. We completely repot the roses about every three years – digging up, pruning, trimming back any damaged roots and replanting in fresh soil-based potting mix – 2 parts topsoil, 1 part peat (moist), ½ part grit or horticultural sand and ½ part rose fertilizer.

For a little bit of restraint (a word not often used in this garden) I enjoy putting a series of pots – using all the same pots filled with all the same plant –in a row. At the start of the canal we have a row of *Dianella tasmanica* (60cm/24in), a member of the phormium family with shiny evergreen leaves. The tiny flowers are followed by gorgeous berries, just like the semi-precious stone lapis lazuli. Try planting up a series of pots all filled with scarlet geraniums, or use box, one of the smaller grasses, sedums, rosemary, and cannas or long-flowering *Geranium* 'Rozanne' (30cm/12in).

Shameless cheating especially applies to potted lilies. As soon as I can get hold of fresh, plump bulbs (this year in mid-January) I pot them up, preferably using clay pots and a soil-based mix. When the buds are just about to open, I plonk them around the garden, wherever they look nice. It's easy to disguise the pot with foliage, and they have to be watered anyway, wherever they are. When the flowers fade, I drag the pots off for the foliage to mature in a corner of the yard. In late

autumn I turn the pots on their sides to stop the bulbs getting sodden. I then repot them in about February.

Potted pelargoniums, fuchsias, begonias and succulents. Stand pots on upturned pots to create height.

Years ago I had a London balcony (3 x 1.5m/ 10 x 5ft), so I know just what happiness gardening in a tiny space can bring. Recently a friend who has gardened for thirty years or more on a sunny Notting Hill balcony was telling me which plants have consistently done well. We're talking true survivors here: plants (or their replacements after disturbances such as house painting) that she still loves and still look good. 'I've tried a million plants,' she tells me, but after so many years she is consistently loyal to the following.

At either end of her balcony are small, very prickly evergreen berberis, to deter intruders from adjoining balconies. Tumbling down over the edge of the balcony 'from day one' is the Moroccan daisy once called *Leucanthemum hosmariense* and now called, two name changes later, *Rhodanthemum hosmariense* (30cm/12in, Z9 but possibly Z8 with perfect drainage), a beautiful mound of lacy silver leaves. Bronze and green fennel 'looks wonderful with rain on it'. Orange-red *Sphaeralcea munroana* (90cm/3ft) grows in boxes that are dry in winter, as they are tucked in right beside the house. Other long-term residents include *Anomatheca laxa* (30cm/12in), a little South African self-seeding bulb; *Osteospermum ecklonis* (1m/3ft), a white daisy with a bright blue middle, an elegant plant compared with the new, squat, over-leafy cultivars; *Mimulus aurantiacus* (90cm/3ft); cannas – 'the one with the red leaf – it goes into the back studio for winter protection'; *Ophiopogon planiscapus* 'Nigrescens' (30cm/12in); *Pelargonium sidoides* (30cm/12in) – silver leaves, small very dark crimson flowers. My friend's favourite plant is *Convolvulus cneorum* (60cm/24in), the beautiful silver-leaved, shrubby cousin of the mad weed. Added to this very select list are various annual poppies (sown in autumn and spring), cobaea – a terrific climber with bell-shaped cup-and-saucer flowers, and single-colour sweet peas (not a packet of mixed colours) that she grows every spring from seed.

MORE SUGGESTIONS FOR POTS
Best vegetables for pots (big pots needed here)
French and runner beans; Swiss chard; cut-and-come-again salads; rocket; courgettes; spring onions; radishes; tomatoes; peppers; herbs.

Shady patios
Aucubas; variegated privet; box; hostas; fatsia (x *Fatshedera lizei*); camellias; sarcococca; London pride (*Saxifraga urbium*) – looks lovely massed on its own; ferns – particularly *Polystichum setiferum* cultivars; tree ferns in sheltered coastal areas; schefflera; francoas, especially the white one; ivies; spider ivy (*Chlorophytum comosum*), a fantastic shade plant in a large hanging basket; fuchsias; hydrangeas; hollies; *Viburnum tinus*, *Choisya ternata*.; and in summer begonias and busy lizzies.

Plants that will tolerate irregular watering
The following all love sun: sempervivums; echeverias; agaves; yuccas; aloes; rosemary; sedums.

To tumble over the edge of a pot
Catmint (*Nepeta*); *Plechostachys serpyllifolia*; *Glechoma hedereacea*; small campanulas; *Clematis* 'Arabella'; *Rubus tricolor*, *Helichrysum petiolare*; verbenas; prostrate rosemary.

Rapid-growing climbers
Cobaea scandens; golden hop (*Humulus lupulus* 'Aureus'); white potato vine (*Solanum laxum* 'Album'); *Jasminum polyanthum*.

Plants for windy balconies
Buddleja; *Atriplex halimus*; hebes; *Elaeagnus* 'Quicksilver'; tamarix; rosemary; phormiums; escallonias; fuchsias.

Good staking

Staking is one of the more subtle arts of gardening. It's not just a question of grabbing a bamboo cane, sticking it in beside a plant and winding a bit of string tightly around the two, which often results in slow torture of the vegetable kind. Staking is potentially a most annoying job: the cane is either too tall or too short, you've forgotten the ties or string, you've forgotten to bring scissors or secateurs to cut the string, you've brought secateurs along but they're a bit blunt and snag the string rather than cut it or, no sooner do you put the cane in, than it snaps off at ground level. Ideally, of course, you would own a small plantation of hazel and birch, from which you would gather suitable twiggy branches that would miraculously blend with the plants they support within a week of insertion. But if, like most of us, it's bamboo canes or nothing, they're much the better for being painted dark green.

Also we find the semicircular metal stakes on two legs terrifically useful. The original templates came from the Somerset garden of Margery Fish. the much-admired writer and gardener, who died in 1969. We took them to Ireland in the 1970s and had them copied by a blacksmith. The sizes we use most often are those with legs of 90cm/3ft, 60cm/24in and 40cm/16in, but we have various other sizes as well – including the odd very tall one. For supporting typical herbaceous plants such as a clump of phlox or heleniums, they are brilliant, and we use them instead of the method of putting in three or four stakes around a clump and tying a piece of string from stick to stick, cat's-cradle style.

Beginners are usually fooled by dahlias. When you put in young plants or tubers, they seem so small that they get a bamboo cane if they're lucky. But dahlias develop into heavy, leafy plants with succulent, easily broken stems. The traditional supports for dahlias were hefty wooden stakes, but we find semicircular metal hoops both excellent and unobtrusive.

Supports comprising a complete circle of metal supported on three legs are very handy for supporting bulky shrubs such as Californian tree poppy (*Romneya coulteri*), shrub roses and beefy perennials such as Joe Pye weed (*Eupatorium purpureum*) and *Silphium perfoliatum* (a whopper of a yellow daisy). Val is superb at staking, and far more patient (with staking, at any rate) than I am.

He has also designed a single metal stake with a curly top (for, say, a tall bearded iris stem) and a circular stake on one leg. The legs of both these supports are of differing heights. Any sloppy staking Val finds, he pounces on immediately and alters. He particularly dislikes very obvious bamboo canes sticking out way above the plant, especially if they're not painted green. (Note: If you can't buy these metal hoops locally, you may have to get them specially made. The problem with some commercially available stakes is the metal's too thin and weak. As Mrs Beeton might say, first catch your blacksmith . . .)

The young birch trees in the front garden arrived bare rooted (and therefore quicker to establish than container-grown trees), so for each we banged a short stake very firmly into the ground (using a heavy lump hammer) before planting. The biggest mistake beginners make is that they use too weak a stake and don't bang them in deeply enough – my stakes are 30–40cm/12–18in in the ground. Wide black plastic ties secure the trees to the stakes, which are on the same side as the prevailing wind so that the bark isn't rubbed during a gale. Container-grown trees need a low stake put in at an angle of 45 degrees. For very slender whippy trees use a temporary, taller stake until roots establish. We secured our large container-grown multi-stem birch with a huge rootball in several places to a short piece of wood that is nailed to two connecting short thick stakes on either side of the tree. For weighty shrubs that need to be secured to a wall, we use strong plastic-covered wire, such as that sold for clothes lines, threaded through sections of old hosepipe to prevent chafing.

The fact that they need good staking is enough to put gardeners off delphiniums. Every year in this garden there's invariably a curious phenomenon, just as our plants are looking more promising than ever, their spires of heart-stoppingly blue flowers on the point of opening. At this moment along comes the Delphinium Wind. We hear it moaning away in the middle of the night and in the morning we can hardly bear to look out of the window.

Anyway, this is how (after years of trial and lots of error) we stake delphiniums. Early in the year, when they are about 45cm/18in high, we support them with a low circular one-legged stake; when they get taller, we enclose the clump completely with two semicircular hoops. At 1.5m/5ft we loosely tie the stems individually to dark green bamboo canes, the tips of which finish a few inches below the top of the flower stem. The stems must not be glued to the canes, as they need room to sway about – tied too tightly they snap off. I'm particularly keen on delphiniums bred by Karl Forster (1874–1970), the celebrated German plantsman. He selected them from thousands of different seedlings and they are slightly shorter, with more slender spires that are less top-heavy (so the plants are more wind tolerant), should flower twice (early summer and autumn) and are all beautiful clear blues (as in 'Berghimmel' and 'Perlmutterbaum'). Undeniably growing delphiniums is a major pain, especially the staking part, but there's no flower that better reminds me of midsummer and I always forget from year to year just how intoxicating is delphinium blue. Just as I use real cotton or linen sheets, I prefer to grow one troublesome delphinium than a hundred easy-care plants.

Clematis

This very morning I dug up a dead clematis. Or rather our gardener Mary did, after we'd decided it was definitely dead. It was the dusky, plump-petalled cousin of the orange-peel clematis, with little nearly black buds, called 'Glasnevin Dusk', which Seamus O'Brien (of the National Botanic Gardens in Dublin) collected as seed in Tibet. The reason for its demise was that I cut it back too hard in the autumn because, charmed as I was by its flowers, its vigorous growth swamped all neighbouring plants. At the same time as I committed this gardening atrocity, I discovered one strange small seedling close by, which I potted up to see what it was. It turned out to be a clematis. Being a typical gardener, I'm either annoyed that a plant is growing too well or furious that it isn't.

Despite their inbuilt death wish, I adore clematis. The large-flowered clematis have irresistible appeal, but at the rate I lose (or kill) them, I've had to accept that most aren't going to be here for long. All my ideas of growing old with my large-flowered clematis are not to be. My attitude now must be here-today-gone-tomorrow. As the garden centres are full of them, I'll go and get another. 'Nelly Moser' (two-tone mauve and pink) was long lived, and so were 'Comtesse de Bouchaud' (germolene pink) and 'Beauty of Worcester' (intense dark blue) – note the past tense for these three; but even 'Jackmanii' (purple), a widely grown so-called easy one, never reached flowering stage, though I tried three times. Even without wilt, which seems widespread, clematis stems are heartbreakingly fragile and their tendrils easily broken. Perhaps it's imagination but it's almost as if they shrink away as I approach.

It could be – and this could apply to the whole buttercup family, the *Ranunculaceae* – that clematis like what old-style gardeners would call 'virgin soil' – rich topsoil that's only ever grown grass, or been ploughed for strictly rotated crops, or been well cared for in a vegetable garden. Soil in old gardens (the garden here has been intensely cultivated since 1830) often suffers from not only a build-up of pests and diseases but also a shortage of plant nutrients. And, in my opinion, just as roses suffer from replant disease (roses planted where others have just been growing rarely flourish), so do clematis. Never plant a new clematis where one has just died. Or perhaps clematis don't thrive here as I should like because they don't like thin gravelly soil and yearn for richer, heavier fare.

Clematis are a marvellously versatile family, from the delectable *C. tenuiloba*, about 15cm/6in tall, with angelic blue flowers, and sweet little spring-flowering creamy-green ones such as *C. x cartmanii* 'Joe', to rollicking May-flowering *C. montana*, always on the rampage, born to cover the ugliest of garden sheds. After all my negative comments, it's good to announce that other spring-flowering species, such as *C. alpina* and *C. macropetala*, are easily available, easy to grow and easy to prune – you don't have to – and do well in this garden. And even the collector's species *C. fusca*, with bell-shaped, funny, furry brown-purple fat little flowers like moles, reappears every year.

There are some clematis that make me happy every time I walk by because they are growing so well: herbaceous *C. integrifolia* (75cm/30in, Z3), with deep blue flowers, vigorous rosy lilac 'Betty Corning', purple-veined 'Venosa Violacea', silver-pink 'Etoile Rose' (one of the *C. texensis* cultivars), 'Propertius', with its flirtatiously turned-up rosy outer petals, and, of course, the incomparable 'Perle d'Azur'.

To plant clematis I dig a hole with minimum measurements of 60 x 60cm/24 x 24 in and the same deep. Then I add a bucket of garden compost and a bucket of fresh soil or peat and leafmould, or all four, plus some general organic fertilizer. Often I just fill the hole with good, fresh topsoil.

Getting the clematis out of its pot is tricky. Sometimes, before upending the pot, it's safer to cut the plant, including the cane it's tied to, down to 15cm/6in from soil level with sharp secateurs. There's nothing worse than trying to get the whole thing out, stake and all, and then watching, almost in slow motion as with most accidents, as the cane falls away, breaking the stem with it. Anyway, for clematis to establish fast, you are meant to cut them back the moment they're planted.

Before planting, soak the pot in a bucket of water for a few minutes. If the roots are congested, tease them gently to loosen them up. Plant, allowing about 2.5cm/1in of the stem to remain below soil level, and firm carefully. This is done to encourage more roots to form. The clematis is extremely vulnerable at this juncture and sometimes I wrap the lower halves of the stems in a sleeve of wire netting about 30cm/12in high and 15cm/6in in diameter or surround them with two to three big stones (not actually touching the stems) to protect them from heedless foot or charging dog. Clematis detest being dry and a section of drainpipe or pot sunk into the ground beside them ensures that any water available from a can reaches the roots. A good thick mulch of garden compost will help keep the roots moist.

Once you've bought a clematis, it's most important not to lose the label: you can then look it up and see what sort of pruning it needs. Large-flowered clematis that bloom in early summer, such as 'Nelly Moser', 'Duchess of Edinburgh', 'Lasurstern' and 'Countess of Lovelace', flower on stems formed the previous year, so you just prune them very lightly by trimming back to the first healthy bud and removing dead wood

We train *Clematis x durandii* (1.5m/5ft) to stakes and plant it in the front of the border within easy reach of the watering can.

Clematis 'Venosa Violacea' is a long-lived cultivar of *C. viticella*.

in late winter. Late-summer-flowering cultivars of *Clematis viticella* – 'Comtesse de Bouchaud' and 'Royal Velours', for example – are cut back to within 60–90cm/2–3ft. If you've forgotten what a clematis is called and cut one of the early-flowering clematis back hard, you'll miss a season's flowering. Conversely, if you don't prune late-flowering clematis, you'll have a lanky plant with flowers too high to enjoy.

Garden visit

I wonder if you've ever had a visit from the two ladies in blue? Navy blue that is, with nice little white blouses and matching navy shoes, handbags and umbrellas. Nuns in mufti, you'd think, and such delicate creatures – they look as if a puff of wind would blow them away. They come from the generation that considers it perfectly OK to collect cuttings in other people's gardens. The sting goes as follows: one sticks her umbrella into the ground close to a desirable plant; they continue to walk round the garden; just as they are about to depart, one of them appears to have forgotten something, returns to fetch the umbrella, hurriedly secretes the plant deep inside and off they go. How could I ever challenge two such exquisite beings anyway? 'Madam, I believe you have one of my plants inside your umbrella' just seems too uncouth.

The 1970s story of the missing meconopsis seed in Branklyn, Perth (owned by the National Trust for Scotland), involved some clever investigative work. Stuart Annand, in charge of the garden at the time, had been waiting to harvest a single ripening pod of the precious poppy. On his daily rounds (for which he always wore a kilt), to his disgust the pod had gone. But beside the plant was a fresh footprint in a recognizable pattern. A couple came into view, the only people in the garden. On a hunch, Stuart remarked to the woman, 'I think you've got something stuck to your shoe,' whereupon she lifted her foot, revealing the telltale design. Following a heated discussion, the pod was handed over.

Graham Stuart Thomas, the great plantsman and writer whom I much admired, used to say that the first time you visit a garden it's important that the weather's nice and you're with friends. If it's a rainy day, your vision of that garden will always be thus.

I love visiting gardens myself. Compare and contrast is the order of the day: some plant at the venue is either bigger and healthier, with many more flowers than mine, or satisfyingly small – for garden outings, always pack a little *Schadenfreude* with your sandwiches. I know myself that the well-placed nettle, about two-thirds of the way round our garden, cheers people up no end (and we used to have hostas near by but we got so tired of people asking about how to control slugs that they had to go).

On visits, how should one comment on some questionable garden feature, such as the large fake bronze fountain depicting two fairies sheltering under an umbrella? I don't know whether 'Gosh' or 'Crikey' is the most appropriate. Both could well be exclamations of delight or astonishment.

Garden visiting has its own unwritten rules: try not to touch the plants – even thoughtfully fingering them can make the owner wince – and don't keep up a running commentary in a loud voice. One of my most memorable group visits included a heavily fortified woman in a brass-buttoned jacket. Pointing at a small tree against the wall (I think it was a variegated azara), she announced to her husband, following close at heel, 'That would do well on the north wing of the kitchen.' She thus informed me, and the other thirty-nine people in her group, that her house was so big that even the kitchen had more than one wing. Gosh.

What to wear on a garden visit? Here the old mac and flat shoes come into their own. If it starts to rain, the more you hang about getting wet the better you prove that you're so used to being outdoors that you haven't noticed. Always carry a notebook and pencil, and if the garden owner tells you the name of something be sure to write it down. (Some people ask questions but don't listen to the answer, and others know the answer very well themselves and are just testing you. They may be one of those fascist greens hoping to catch you out on the subject of insecticide or herbicide – not that I use either, but I'm pretty hot on the fungicide). You may notice that in groups, even small ones, one person is the self-elected leader and however much the rest of the party manoeuvres to get by, even to the extent of stepping on to flowerbeds beside narrow paths, they never succeed in doing so. The leader does all the talking, gets the best view of the garden and manages to exhibit a grand display of horticultural knowledge to anyone within earshot.

In a garden that feels good you'll often find its owner working in it, and the welcome you get will stay with you until you leave. The foundation of a truly happy visit is the interaction between you, the garden and its owner. I reckon there's something to learn about in every garden – a new plant, a pleasing grouping of plants or an inspiring piece of design that could be adapted for use at home. Don't forget to take the sun and the good friends with you. And, of course, the sandwiches.

The great May rush

The most active and physically demanding gardening happens in late May. There's so much to do that I get distracted and begin too many things and forget to finish them. I can hardly move in the greenhouse without knocking something over, and then I trip over something else on the way to get the brush and dustpan. I can almost see the plants growing on warm days as the temperature soars and seedlings everywhere are yearning to escape the kitchen windowsill, the bathroom, the hot press (airing cupboard) and the greenhouse. The alpine house offers some space for plants to be hardened off properly, but more often than not plants must be shoved outside straight from the steaming warm greenhouse to take their chance in the notoriously flippant May weather. Many pots and trays of plants spend the day outside and go back inside for the night.

Suddenly the bluebells fade. To stop them seeding, we yank handfuls of stems out of the ground, straight from the bulb, and dump them on the compost heap. The gentle blue haze of forget-me-nots is also disappearing and I'm rapidly tiring of them. Pretty as they are, forget-me-nots are good at secreting themselves in the cool shade under the leaves of herbaceous plants and making a nuisance of themselves next spring. The miserable, squinny little forget-me-not that infests this garden is one of the Irish native species, rather than the cultivated form gone wild. Every few years, for neat little plants with proper bright blue flowers, I try to throw out all the old ones and start again with freshly grown seedlings.

The big dahlia planting takes place about the third week in May. Even in Ireland that's taking a risk, but by then I can't stand the congestion in the greenhouse. David Shackleton used to say that it wasn't safe to plant out tender stuff until the second week in June. (So much for the local supermarkets and hardware shops, which have been displaying their busy lizzies and begonias and other tender plants since March.) Mary and I begin by placing vivid red *Dahlia* 'Murdoch' at intervals along the red border. We potted these hefty plants into largeish pots in autumn, kept them in the shed for winter and watered them about once a month until February and then about once a week; then we brought them into the greenhouse in March and hardened them off (days outside, nights inside) for two weeks before planting them. We put in stakes at the same time as

the plants, because although dahlias look sturdy enough, they can rapidly develop into heavy, lush plants that will topple over as soon as you look the other way.

For thirty years or so I left dahlias in the ground over winter. No plants died, but now I reckon we get a better, earlier show from stored tubers. Whereas we plant out the big, old plants now, we grow smaller plants from spring cuttings, which will be wonderful for filling in gaps in late June or July. Cuttings are easy – you must try them. As soon as the shoots are about 10cm/4in high, cut them off cleanly below a leaf joint or with a tiny slice of tuber and insert into a cutting mix – I often use half vermiculite, half peat. Keep in moist, warm, light conditions shaded from direct sun.

Next to be positioned and planted are the cannas, particularly *Canna* 'Musifolia', which is the tallest we have and a cracking good big-leaved plant.

A late May day goes something like this: drag trays of runner bean seedlings and big pots of *Salvia confertiflora* (2m/7ft) out of greenhouse; walk round garden spotting gaps and wondering what to fill them with; chop back rosemary that's squashing dasylirion; water greenhouse and newly planted dahlias; go to garden centre and buy some tuberous begonias that I don't need at all; find forgotten pot of *Centaurea* 'Jordy' (45cm/18in) hidden under an iris; feel deeply guilty, cut it back, soak it in water and plant in half-decent position; spoil delphiniums on the point of bloom with yet another watering; dig up last of tulips (making sure to pick up fallen petals as well, as they can spread tulip fire disease); squidge greenfly infestation on rose 'Rhapsody in Blue'; nip back capsid-bug-bitten growing shoots (8cm/3in) of *Salvia uliginosa* (2m/7ft) – I do this to many plants to remove pests and encourage more flowers at the same time; damp down (swill lots of water on tiled floor of) greenhouse to reduce temperature and increase humidity; cut away old snail-eaten leaves from phormium and beschorneria; find a forest of epilobium seedlings, no time to get gloves from shed, make hands even worse than usual by pulling them out; water and tie in clematis 'Betty Corning'; pick deadheads off bearded irises; pinch out tips of a third of each clump of phlox and heleniums to prolong blooming; pick first flowers from sweet peas sown last autumn to enjoy heavenly scent in house and stop seed forming (which stops flowering); pick caterpillars off pelargonium in greenhouse; drag runner bean seedlings and pots of salvias back into greenhouse and shut door; have gloat over lime-green umbellifer, *Mathiasella bupleuroides* 'Green Dream' (90cm/3ft), a present from Bob Brown of Cotswold Garden Flowers; have bath.

When you are putting out your tender summer plants you'll have more success if you dig and prepare a whole patch (90cm/3ft square, say) and plant it all in one go. You'll be planting young plants, all at the same stage of growth, to compete with each other. But if you dig a hole in the middle of established plants, it will be like putting a junior in among the prefects at school – the roots of the big boys will move in and the new plant won't have a hope.

Mathiasella bupleuroides 'Green Dream'

Part 3

FANCY STUFF

Exotic planting

Perhaps it is a natural revolt against Edwardian gardens, Jekyllian herbaceous borders flowing with sensitively arranged colours, white gardens and box parterres. Perhaps it is an instinctive rebellion against gardens so themed that they're almost Disney-like, no garden being complete without its decorative vegetable garden, rose garden, heritage herbs, annual border and wildflower meadow. But then exotic planting, the canna–banana garden, arrived, with as much cheek and chutzpah as a spotty youth arriving at a cocktail party. Gardeners from London to Dublin and San Francisco could hear the distinct rumble of the collapsing pyramid of good taste. Suddenly every pair of box balls announcing the entrance to every lavender-edged path into every rose garden seemed unutterably smug, and the cat got sick on every Lutyens bench that ever saluted a piece of paving fetchingly colonized with carpets of thyme. Terrific. Roll on the revolution.

Agreed, I'm as guilty as the next for following these fashions, but once the sneaky feeling has crept in, there's nothing so much fun as throwing buns at the ideas of the past one hundred years of gardening. Christopher Lloyd became, of course, the leader in bucking the trend when he dug up his whole rose garden and replanted it with a scintillating array of dramatic-looking, mostly tender plants.

Hedychiums or ginger lilies are especially valuable for their showy leaves and flowers. You may know *Hedychium gardnerianum* (2m/7ft), the tall sweetly scented late-summer-flowering conservatory plant. This is listed as zone 8, but I don't think it's as hardy as *H. forrestii* (1.2m/4ft), listed as zone 9, which has thrived outdoors for many years here. In cold winters its fleshy rhizomes near the soil's surface go mushy, but some survive at a lower level, to surface in late May, as great fat satiny shiny red shoots. Because you get all the effects of handsome canna-like leaves, without having to dig it up and store it for winter, I have it planted in four different places. With a thick autumn mulch you'd get away with it in considerably colder gardens. *Hedychium coccineum* 'Tara' (1.2m/4ft) is another favourite, not only for its orange flowers but also for the blue-green leaves. This has been extremely slow

We give the Chusan palm (*Trachycarpus fortunei*) lots of tomato fertilizer, so it flowers well.

Joe Pye weed, cannas, fuchsias, roses and lobelia with the large green paddles of *Canna* 'Musifolia'

(around twenty years) to get going, but I've just replanted it in a rich pie of old manure and compost. We leave some plants of *H. greenei* (1.5m/5ft), with its bronze-backed leaves, to overwinter outside, but we dig up others and store them in frost-free conditions. I love having a few hedychiums or cannas in large pots to use for filling late gaps. Shrubby *Tibouchina urvilleana* (2m/7ft), with large velvety violet flowers, spends summers outside plunged in the border, pot and all. This must be watered daily and moved back under glass before the first frost. Pinch it out regularly to keep it bushy. *Tibouchina grandifolia* (2.5m/8ft) from Brazil, with luscious soft foliage and royal blue flowers, is a new acquisition. Both are easy from cuttings.

Tetrapanax papyrifer (3m/10ft) the ricepaper plant (rice paper is extracted from the pith of the stem), has highly ornamental big leaves, and the cultivar 'Rex' is a superb plant, with even bigger felted leaves. I make a special protective winter cage for its stem and vulnerable growing point, a column over 90cm/3ft tall made out of a bubble-wrap and wire-netting sandwich, and keep a spare young plant in the greenhouse, just in case.

We also wrap our banana (*Musa basjoo*, 5m/16ft) for winter. I've seen that even where bananas are grown as a crop the leaves are usually wind tattered. Ours takes weeks to look as if it's really

enjoying life in Dublin. That's why I'm so fond
of *Canna* 'Musifolia' (1.8m/6ft; the cultivar

Cannas and begonias fill a gap that had tulips in spring.

name means 'with leaves like a banana'), which we planted out only this week (early June). The foliage is still in good condition despite recent high winds. I'm told that this cultivar never blooms, although it did once have rather measly red flowers. So what – this is a wonderful plant for height and leafy presence. I adore soft apricot orchid lookalike *Canna* 'Panache' (1.2m/4ft), which for those of sensitive taste doesn't even look like a canna.

Many cabbage trees or cordylines grow in Dublin. People think they are palms but in fact they are members of the agave family. True palms that do well here include *Trachycarpus fortunei* (20m/65ft), the Chusan palm from subtropical Asia, and the European *Chamaerops humilis* (4m/12ft). If I were to begin the garden again, I'd choose the latter, because the more silvery leaves are stiffer and don't get so bashed about by wind. Because of being bad at geography (when I was aged about twelve, the geography mistress remarked that I didn't seem to like geography, and I was allowed to give it up then and there), I used to think that palms lived in the desert on little other than sand, but I now understand that they enjoy the occasional feed.

Gardening in old age

Gardening in old age should be full of joy, just like gardening as a child. Children are never conscious of how time is flying along, never worry whether or not the lawn needs mowing, think flowers and weeds are equally beautiful and all insects equally fascinating, and never have thoughts such as 'This same flower that smiles today will be dying tomorrow.' For later life you should plan your garden so that gardening is of the most tranquil kind, with masses of time for sitting and thinking how lovely everything is, without being harassed by urgent gardening chores.

It's said that gardening is all about control; but perhaps the secret of gardening in old age is giving in to certain plants, letting them stretch their roots and spread, letting them have their wayward ways and if one beautiful plant is madly colonizing the whole area, letting it be. It is worth finding out which plants are strong enough to coexist with the wild runners, the incontinent self-seeders and the rampant climbers. Think of your newfound wilderness as different layers of planting, from early bulbs to June poppies, prairie daisies and asters, Japanese anemones and colchicums – all the plants that revel in competition.

And another thing you can give up controlling is the lawn. Just think of the quantities of thought, time, expense, frustration and heavy repetitive work involved in presenting a perfect green sward. No sooner do you complete the cycle of mowing, edging, feeding and watering – not to mention aeration and worrying about the moss – than you start all over again. It was for that reason that we dug up two lawns, one to make the canal, another to make a gravel garden.

'But I do love grass,' I hear you argue. So do I, and all our yesterdays probably include sitting on a rug on a daisy-covered lawn. But you could reduce the amount of grass that must be cut by mowing only a wide path really short (the course of which could be changed at any moment) and leaving the remainder for bulbs and wild flowers. You could also grow lots of grasses to make up for lack of lawn, such as *Stipa tenuissima* (60cm/24in), *Calamagrostis brachytricha* (90cm/3ft) and *Oryzopsis miliacea*. (This last is a brilliant, shimmering, delicate grass 90cm/3ft tall which looks good for most of the year and is perfect for gardens in a temperate climate, where it produces just the right amount of seedlings. I'm told it's invasive in hotter countries.)

Stipa tenuissima isn't very long lived, but seeds gently about.

Back to control: much of my gardening time has been taken up with stopping vigorous plants from annexing smaller ones. Think of all the lovely, easy plants that spread at the roots such as the pale pink and white form of rosebay willow herb, doronicums, evening primroses, old-fashioned alstroemerias (the smart new hybrids have better manners) and many bamboos, not to mention all those flowers that spread by seed. But whereas ten years ago I dug up all plants that responded to this garden with a joyous ramp, I now permit many to stay. Long may they flourish. And instead of replacing difficult plants when they die – those I've tried to grow for a quarter of a century, such as hardy orchids, large-flowered clematis (I've an alarming record for losing these) and delicate, tricky alpines – I'm falling in love all over again with easy, common plants, such as pot marigolds, the white form of valerian (*Centranthus ruber* 'Albus'), foxgloves, candytuft and *Erigeron karvinskianus*, a little pink and white daisy, a completely self-catering plant.

One of the most important considerations for old age (to call it by its proper name instead of a euphemism – I noticed on a recent visit to the USA that even a dog was referred to either as 'an older dog' or 'a senior dog') is what calibre of help will be available. The English mixed border is arguably the most complicated sort of gardening there is, involving an intricate balance of height,

Catananche caerulea and *Stipa tenuissima*

colour, season, space and available nutrients. Furthermore, mixed borders in an old garden, where many layers of elaborate planting reflect the owner's changing taste, are even more daunting to gardening help. If you think about most of the grand Italian and French gardens, with their parterres, hedges and wide expanses of grass, they don't require gardeners with great knowledge to mow, clip or tidy. Thus I'm trying to divide this garden into areas that need little upkeep, and if they do, a general-maintenance gardener paid by the hour will be fine for them, and smaller, intensely planted patches for plants that need lots of attention from me or Val or Mary. And of course there's always a sneaking awareness that there may be no help at all.

Simplifying the planting requires steely resolve. Here are a few examples of plants I no longer grow, and why: hostas – except for two, 'Sum and Substance' and 'Snowden' (because of slugs); heucheras (vine weevil are addicted to them); caryopteris (too subject to capsid bug); *Robinia pseudoacacia* (too brittle, branches fall off in gales); many roses (virulent blackspot); *Sisyrinchium striatum* 'Aunt May' (always cluttered with dead black leaves); variegated blackberry (ugly); *Brunnera macrophylla* 'Dawson's White' (white variegated sections of leaves burnt in dry weather); several peonies (roots too vulnerable to swift moth larvae); *Rubus cockburnianus* (invasive terrorist).

I confess that the principal reason I stop growing something is either that I no longer like it or that it has become too large. I still cannot resist delphiniums, for their heavenly blue, troublesome and unfashionable as they are. I've always adored self-seeding plants, the great survivors, that so charmingly position themselves with no work from me: opium poppies; love-in-a-mist; honesty; perennial stock; candytuft; foxgloves; *Campanula persicifolia* and *C. lactiflora*; columbines; teasels; many alliums (decorative onions); valerian; double Welsh poppies (*Meconopsis cambrica*) – we remove any single ones the moment they bloom; larkspur; angel's fishing rods or dierama; nasturtiums; and a million and one of prickly Miss Wilmott's ghost (*Eryngium giganteum*).

I suspect that the older one gets the more serenity is needed. A couple of years ago when we got rid of all the fidgety planting in the front garden – one of this and one of that – we replaced the area with fresh soil before planting our fifty-one birch trees. This new soil had a magical effect on my snowdrops and erythroniums, moved from the back garden to grow under the birch. At last they are recovering their vigour. I am attempting (not easy for an incorrigible plant enthusiast) to have simple planting in front of the house: *Astrantia major* 'Buckland' (75cm/30in), one of the best of the masterworts, with greenish pink flowers and a good autumn display; another umbellifer, *Seseli libanotis* (90cm/3ft), which looks like a green cow parsley but isn't so invasive; lots of *Aster divaricatus* (60cm/24in); *Euphorbia stygiana* (1.5m/5ft), *Beschorneria yuccoides* (1.2m/4ft), *Aloe striatula* (1.75m/6ft), sarcococca, *Pulmonaria* 'Diana Clare' (40cm/15in), pale blue columbines, astelias and grasses. In the sunny areas there are dieramas, and a quiet mix of aunty colours, including brownish purple *Allium sphaerocephalon* (90cm/3ft) mixed with faded grey-blue *Catananche caerulea* (90cm/3ft). We mulched the whole area with 10cm/4in of grey gravel (we used no horticultural fabric and the soil was clean of perennial weeds). Barely ten minutes' work has been done on the whole area for the past six months – just some hand-watering in dry weather and a quick tidy of faded bulb foliage. Now not only does the view from the front door present a peaceful view, with fluttering birch leaves catching the light, but also the garden there feels calm and restful, as there's little maintenance.

For old age I'd like a bench on a slope facing the evening sun with a honeysuckle growing near by, smooth paths that I could glide along with nothing to trip over, so I'd never fall over and be stuck like an upside-down beetle. But most of all I'd like to see a family of newly fledged long-tail tits practising their first bath in the old font.

Greenhouse

A frost-free, five-star showcase for tender plants, a nursery for seedlings, intensive care for delicate plants, a propagation parlour for cuttings – a greenhouse is all these things, but most important for me is the peace of the place, however much harassment stalks outside.

On blustery summer days when the Delphinium Wind is raging, the plants are wilting and I'm cross, I shelter in the greenhouse. On cold days, I begin the day with a visit for a quick warm-up and a look at the cuttings under the bell jar to see how they're getting on – they usually look remarkably similar to how they did the previous day, but I like looking anyway. Have you ever noticed how quiet and still plants are in midwinter? They are silent, immobile, their life almost at a standstill. Whereas in the heat of summer, when I come in with the watering can and plants are dry and thirsty, their leaves seem to quiver with expectation. Watch and see.

Practicalities: our first greenhouse, built *circa* 1974, was of softwood painted white. We used plate glass for the doors and sides, as I'd once fallen through a glass door, after which I had major respect for glass. (I looked so wrecked after the accident, with twenty-five stitches, that a man on a number 19 London bus remarked that I'd probably been just a pretty face before.) This greenhouse went the way of all softwood greenhouses and collapsed in the 1990s. We rebuilt it in hardwood, using the same glass. We used no wood preservative, as we wanted the timber to fade to silver. There are ten small windows and two doors – getting a greenhouse built involves a lot of arguments with the builder, during which you'll continue to explain that plants need a great deal of air. We have electric heating, which may not be the cheapest but is easy to manage with a thermostat, set at about 5°C/42°F. There is an easily cleaned tiled floor and a bed of soil the whole length of the back wall for plants that don't enjoy being confined to a pot. Occupying a lime-free section about 1m/3ft square is *Lapageria rosea*, the national flower of Chile, which they say is the most beautiful climber in the world, with voluptuously cool, rose pink bells.

The greenhouse greatly extends the range of plants I can grow. Here *Canna* 'Musifolia', *Chlorophytum* and *Pelargonium* 'Ardens' crowd against the window.

It doesn't matter how naff or rickety your greenhouse is: any kind of protected area immediately expands your palette of plants by creating different climates. Even with a standard garden shed and a sunny porch you can overwinter many plants – some of my cannas and dahlias spend winter in an outdoor lavatory shed.

The small, paved area just outside the greenhouse is a useful spot for fuchsias, camellias and so on to overwinter as well as pots of seeds that require a cold period to germinate. During the hectic rush of the late spring hardening-off period all areas, especially the alpine house, are crammed with trays and pots constantly being shifted about.

I've always loved what we call geraniums; they're such lovely, cheerful, easy plants. Correctly known as pelargonium, the common old red geranium is one of the Zonal pelargoniums, which often have darker patterns on the leaves, and the big frilly-flowered ones are known as Regal pelargoniums (and also Martha Washington geraniums in the USA).

Regals are happier under glass the whole year except for a few weeks after flowering in late July and August when we deadhead them, cut them back a bit and park them outdoors in a sheltered sunny position for a rest. But Zonals, ivy-leaved and scented-leaved kinds are fine outdoors for summer. I can never decide which I like best, but I adore the ones with scented leaves, especially the rose-scented 'Attar of Roses' – to crush and sniff a leaf is most reviving.

Great loves of the moment (but this will change) include *Pelargonium sidoides* (30cm/12in, scalloped silver-velvet leaves, dark crimson small flowers) and *P*. 'Ardens' (jewel-like dazzling red little flowers, unexciting leaves). This latter is uncommon, probably because of the fact that it's slow to propagate. Shirley Beatty, who's making a new garden (after leaving her wonderful garden, which she had to abandon after forty years because of encroaching high-rise apartments), told me about the slightly peculiar propagation method for 'Ardens', the stems of which have funny bulbous bits from whence the leaves emerge: take short cuttings, including this bulbous bit and bury the cutting, leaves and all, at the bottom of a small pot of cutting mix. With luck you'll have a plant in three to six months' time. At no stage disturb the pot to see what's happening.

In March or April I remove some of the pelargoniums' old potting compost, and trim their roots before repotting them in a soil-based potting mix plus slow-release fertilizer. I take cuttings in March and late August.

I often sort the greenhouse through, plant by plant, deciding whether the plants need repotting or not, shuffling their pots about, sometimes promoting them to first-class positions in the sunny front row, sometimes to the shade on the floor. Every Sunday from April until late September I give nearly everything a liquid feed. Every visit to the greenhouse involves deadheading and tweaking any yellowing leaves, in summer for aesthetic reasons and in winter to help prevent the spread of fungus. In late spring and early summer I do a lot of pinching out, either with secateurs or with finger and thumb. If you nip away the growing tip of the leader, or largest central shoot, and any tips of the side branches, you will cause a plant to bush out, thereby producing a more

compact and floriferous plant. In summer I   *Pelargonium 'Ardens'*
swill down the floor to increase humidity and
lower the temperature, but in winter I sweep it with a dry brush, as water slopped around then is
too encouraging for the fungus botrytis. Each November I congratulate myself that there's no
botrytis, but by December it invariably turns up.

Self-seeders

Undeserved credit is the sweetest. You've done nothing whatsoever to earn it. All the ideas that arrive in the middle of the night to be chewed over in the small hours might never be remarked on, whereas a sublimely placed self-sown foxglove, backlit by the western sun . . . now you're talking.

Of course if it is a white foxglove, I did do something: I make sure that only white seedlings reach maturity by taking out all the pink ones. It's easy to tell which these are, even when the plants are tiny, by looking at the back of the leaf stalk – if you want white only there shouldn't be the faintest trace of pink. I also always stake a few white-flowered plants to make sure that these are the only plants I allow to drop seed, and in July I gather up self-sown white seedlings and fatten them in big trays. As we clean up the garden for winter, spaces appear and there's room for the young plants to go in. (Note: You can't grow foxgloves year after year in the same place, as they fail to thrive. When they're growing wild they move on by seed to fresh areas, just as primroses do. If you go down to the wooded place where you once saw a bank of primroses and foxgloves they probably won't be there, having probably moved just around the corner.)

Gardens are at their most seductive when colonized by self-sown seedlings. I love imagining how the seeds got there. Did they float along on an individual parachute? Burst out from a brittle-ripe seedpod? Attach themselves with viscous liquid to a travelling insect? Or perhaps they were gobbled up and duly expelled by a blackbird. Then there is the story about the traveller in Nepal who sowed his socks when he got home after wearing them for a month-long trek through monsoon weather at low altitude to ice and snow at 5200m/17,000 feet on the border with Tibet. Many never-to-be-identified small seedlings appeared.

Euphorbia lathyris (1.2m/4ft) never ceases to fascinate people, but when you announce that it's officially a weed, their interest cools. It is especially beautiful when the sun shines through the luminous pale green leaves. I love its sculptural shape, which will add presence and interest to any old corner, sun or shade. On

Self-seeded foxgloves have skipped into the blue border, to join the delphiniums and honey-scented seakale flowers.

Self-sown *Erigeron karvinskianus*, teasels, *Eryngium giganteum*, *Seseli libanotis* (like cow parsley, but perennial) and angel's fishing rods

dry warm days the sharp, cracking sound of it 'shooting' seeds, as the dry pods burst open, makes you jump. Pull out any plants showing signs of developing rust disease, depicted by orange pustules developing on the backs of the leaves. (Excellent word, 'pustules', especially when repeated very slowly when feeling irritable.) This handsome biennial always had the reputation of deterring moles, of the tunnelling furry variety, but some say it's an effective treatment for warts.

One of the lovable plants that you only have to buy one packet of seed for in a lifetime's gardening is candytuft or annual iberis. It spreads rapidly but is never a nuisance, as extra seedlings are whisked out in a second. Requirements are sun, poor soil and sporadic neglect. Every year we have a brilliant candytuft moment, with ribbons of colour – white, pale pink and a few lipstick colours thrown in – running in and out of low-growing permanent plants. Flower colour doesn't last long, but the seedheads are remarkably pretty, interlocking whorls of emerald, worthy of smart florists' shops, remaining decorative for many weeks. You also only have to buy one packet of seed of annual self-sowing love-in-a-mist (nigella), which has a lacy ruff of filigree foliage framing blue flowers that are followed by inflated seedpods.

Meconopsis cambrica flore-pleno (60cm/24in), the double form of the Welsh poppy, makes a terrific, long-flowering garden plant. Apart from typical yellow, this also comes with flowers in a lovely light red and a vibrant orange, the colour of fizzy orange drink, making me think of chilly beach picnics and packets of crisps. It's vital to remove every plant with single flowers, unless you're allowing them to colonize a wild area, because if left to its own devices the Welsh

poppy rapidly changes gear into takeover mode. When removing plants, use a sharp trowel and try to dig up the whole, carroty root. As I've been weeding out single poppies

When we first came here the opium poppies were mostly a wishy-washy mauve. It's taken years of only allowing the best shades to seed to achieve these vivid colours.

for many years I get a good proportion of doubles. To be sure they are doubles, you must wait until they flower.

Erigeron karvinskianus (60cm/24in, Z7) is a pretty small daisy from Mexico and Central America with white flowers that fade to soft pink, which manages to locate itself with perfect serendipity in sunny, narrow gaps in paving or walls. I don't think I've ever seen this plant for sale, as nobody would want to buy such a weedy-looking, frail little thing. If it gets a bit above itself, cut it back hard. I've been told this butter-wouldn't-melt-in-the-mouth small daisy is a serious weed in warmer climates.

Perhaps the most irresistible aspect of gardening, for me at any rate, is the way seedlings turn up and position themselves with such blissful happenstance. There they are – teasels, pot marigolds, white musk mallows, heart's-ease (Johnny-jump-ups) or purple-leaved violets. All these lovely things, all undeniably charming, all growing and flowering and making me happy without a teaspoon of effort from me.

Unsettling remarks

I mind very much whether or not I like somebody. The moment I meet them I'm weighing up their charm or lack of it and giving them imaginary points for this or that. My French sister-in-law, on the other hand, has an attitude totally French: as far as she's concerned, if they're amusing company, she couldn't care less, even if they've got piggy eyes and spill their dinner all down their front.

However, when it comes to gardens one of the joys of visiting is that you can have a perfectly lovely time in a garden you don't much like. You can eavesdrop on observations about plants, such as 'I've got one at home – but mine's bigger.' In a garden north of London and west of Oxford, I overheard the comment 'Of course she throws money at her garden' – and then, after a long pause, 'But she does it impeccably.' However flattering the afterthought, by then the wasp had already stung.

One Sunday two undistinguished women arrived here, age indeterminate. They examined the plants intently, studying them leaf by leaf. I was gratified by how carefully they wrote down the Latin names. Professional women, I decided. Respectable. They were here for ages; I was flattered that they'd found so much of interest. During the afternoon I had dug up a piece of a frilly hart's tongue fern at the end of the garden and, much later, I decided I'd go back and water it. As I went up the path, my eye caught a flash of white. These were professional women of another kind: one was perched (as a lookout, presumably) on the edge of the raised bed and the other, head down and legs wide apart, was enthusiastically shovelling pieces of my plants into a large black plastic bag. I was so annoyed I could barely splutter, 'What on earth . . .' They seemed surprised I had challenged them. It was only then I realized that from the beginning their close encounters with my plants had been of the predatory kind – they were merely pinpointing suitable 'slips' for propagation purposes.

Visitors often comment on how much work there is. A whispered 'She doesn't do it herself, you know' is no doubt comforting to the speaker, but one look at my hands should persuade her otherwise. Garden work is the whole point: I just love doing it, even staking and sweeping and washing pots. The garden is a great outdoor playground in which I hugely enjoy myself; it allows my thoughts to get lost in simple earthy, occupations and to wander off in innocent directions, such as wondering what to plant where and when or whether it's going to rain.

Planting in layers

I'd like to say that most of my efforts to plant in layers for succession of colour have been the result of making notes and plans, but in reality the best interplanting has been the result of a mixture of happy accident and the plants themselves, over many years, dictating where they want to grow and which plants they'd like to mix with.

Early-flowering bulbs are the first layer. For mixing with herbaceous perennials, which sometimes need dividing, choose easy bulbs that tolerate regular disturbance, even being replanted upside down. Thousands of *Crocus tommasianus* (12cm/5in) live in the borders here, plus scillas, muscari, chionodoxas, wood anemones (*Anemone nemorosa*, 15cm/6in) and special forms of celandine (*Ranunculus ficaria*, 10cm/4in), some of which re-establish by seed or root as fast as I disturb them.

One of the great moments of the gardening year is when a thousand crocus simultaneously unfurl their petals to the sun's warmth and the garden is suddenly alight with sheets of luminous mauve. Moment is the word, as the Dublin February sun only reaches the borders around midday and has gone by half past two, and of course there's no show if it rains. I adore these ordinary crocus, but serious plant collectors consider them weeds because they so rapidly colonize an area.

I have lots of small daffodils, such as 'Hawera', 'February Silver', 'Tête-à-tête', *Narcissus rupicola*, Queen Anne's double daffodil (*N.* 'Eystettensis'), *N. bulbocodium* and many more. To start with I fell into the classic beginner's trap of ordering ugly big trumpet daffodils such as 'King Alfred', the super-size-me of all narcissus, which I proceeded to plant in a row beside the path, where their leaves died a very public death. You can't take off the leaves for six weeks after flowering, to nourish the bulb for the following year. If you're growing bulbs in beds (as opposed to naturalizing them in grass), the nearer the back of the bed they're planted the better, as the new foliage of emerging perennials will disguise the fading leaves.

Our main spring border, to the left of the garden as you look out of the window of the house, has something of interest from late January, when there are snowdrops and hellebores, until July. Interplanted with the first bulbs are small early herbaceous plants such as lungworts (pulmonaria),

Pale blue wood anemones (or Wooden Enemies as they're sometimes known), erythroniums, narcissus, tulips and muscari. Hedychiums and the ricepaper plant (*Tetrapanax papyrifer*) follow on in summer.

omphalodes and toothworts (dentaria, correctly cardamine, cousin of our native lady's smock, *Cardamine pratensis*); also – I can't understand why everyone doesn't grow this – *Lathyrus vernus*. About 30cm/12in high, it makes a neat clump and has a non-stop procession of sweet little pea flowers for six weeks in spring, usually in magenta purple, but you can also get lovely pink and white forms. It doesn't mind how much it becomes overshadowed in summer, when the leaves go tacky anyway and you don't want it in too prominent a position.

Following the early spring display is an eight-week satisfactory no-need-for-any-maintenance show of cheerful yellow daisies on the 90cm/3ft stems of the great leopard's bane (*Doronicum pardalianches*, 1.2m/4ft), a European and British native (I'm told it comes from the border counties of England and Scotland). This runs a bit but is very easy to pull up. Intermixed are hundreds of *Nectaroscordum siculum* (1.2m/4ft), which has umbels of little bellflowers in subtle mauve-green colouring on 90cm/3ft stems. As the flowers of this close relation of the allium are fertilized, the seedheads ripen to a straw-coloured sticky-up shape, which reminds me of little turrets of fairy castles. I've only allowed these to seed twice in thirty years. The last ingredient of the late spring self-perpetuating panorama is the self-seeding British native *Aconitum napellus* subsp. *napellus*

Anglicum Group (1.2m/4ft), with its dark blue flowers. Perhaps this happy association of native plants and the decorative but potentially invasive nectaroscordum, all mixed with a mass of early spring bulbs and honesty, is the essence of carefree gardening.

On the other side of the garden, my Californian tree poppy (*Romneya coulteri*, 2.5m/8ft), grows in a very dry spot near a sunny wall. This sensational plant took no less than eight years to establish and produce its beautiful flowers, with crinkled white silky petals. The flowers have a strange scent, hard to describe, except to say that there's a subtle change between the sweetness of the young, just opened flowers and the almost sullen perfume of the older flowers. Once it has its roots down, it can seriously travel; just down the road a shoot appeared in its astonished owner's kitchen. In January we prune the romneya in two different ways: we cut the rear stems to about 1.5m/5ft and prune the front stems to about 30cm/12in – like the British army, shortest to the front, tallest to the rear, which gives us a graduated display of poppy flowers. Romneya makes a good mother plant: under her skirts (which have now expanded in all directions) grow hellebores, perennial honesty (*Lunaria rediviva*), snowdrops and daffodils; rose 'Souvenir de Saint Anne's' is inextricably tied up with the romneya, as is rose 'Henri Martin'; mauve goblets of colchicums appear underneath it in autumn, followed by shiny bright green leaves, wonderful in winter and hidden by the tree poppy when they are doing their messy dying off in June.

Aconitum napellus subsp. *napellus* Anglicum Group and yellow *Doronicum pardalianches*

Corydalis solida (12cm/5in) has pale pinky mauve flowers and blue-green lacy leaves, and a short but welcome season above ground before vanishing underground in May to rest. Every time you disturb the soil near it more of the orange tubers are spread around. Not to be planted near special small plants, as it could swamp them, but it is an easy, pretty plant tolerant of general gardening abuse. Here it provides delicate early colour in the same spot as late-emerging (June) *Arisaema candidissimum* (40cm/16in) and roscoeas. There are several special forms of this corydalis, such as sugar pink 'Beth Evans' and deep coral 'George Baker', but these I keep a careful eye on in raised beds.

Builders' big black plastic bucket

Apart from my small fork with the long handle, the tool I'm most attached to is one of my identical collection of at least thirty builders' big black plastic buckets. (There can be some confusion here if you put the word builders' in the wrong place.) When we began the garden here I used to fling the weeds over my shoulder and leave them around in wilting heaps, with joyous disregard for mess and the person who would have to tidy up. Now I never leave the shed without the bucket; long may the Queen and Mrs Thatcher have their handbags, but for me it will always be the bucket.

My extravagant use of the bucket is not so much laziness as avoidance of work. I've learned that if I go up the garden I'm guaranteed to notice something that needs cutting back, deadheading, weeding, digging up, pinching out, whatever, involving bits and pieces of garden detritus that must be gathered up. To go round picking it up later is unnecessary work. Secateurs, trowel, scissors, ties and sometimes a plastic saucer of chicken pellet fertilizer or fish, blood and bone already in the bucket save expeditions back to the shed. The bucket can be upturned over a recent transplant to protect it from sun, used as a makeshift umbrella in sudden storms or turned upside down to sit on. We need bucket after bucket of compost for planting or mulching, of topsoil for planting (or to be put on top of the mulch to weight it down to stop the blackbirds pulling it out on to the paths) and of gravel for topping up bare patches on gravelled areas or adding to the soil for extra drainage.

The sort of bucket you need, a cheap and honest plastic bucket, can be found in farm shops and builders' merchants. You don't need any of those fancy weed carriers and trugs, for sale in shops not a million miles from Sloane Square, where would-be gardeners marooned for a hot weekend in London buy gardening stuff to cheer themselves up, wistfully wishing they'd been asked to the country for the weekend.

Dog in the garden

I felt like writing to 'Dear Mary', who advises on how to behave in delicate social situations on the back page of *The Spectator*. Last year, the moment the doorbell signalled the arrival of an ambassador and his wife for lunch, Daisy the dachshund puppy did a couple of elegant sausages on the drawing-room floor. Inevitably these became stuck to the ambassadorial shoes, and were trodden towards the door and down the steps to the garden, in a series of telltale footprints. Nothing was said. Nothing was noticed. Correct procedure, I presume.

We adore our dogs, miniature wire-haired dachshunds Mr Reginald and Daisy, but how is it that when we have a large group of visitors, one of them is certain to feel an urgent need to crap? Directly in the middle of the path. Perhaps it's in anticipation of the tea-and-biscuit session in the dining room, where there's a chance of a dropped biscuit organized

Mr Reginald, dachsund

by the god who looks after little dogs. Anyway, what all dogs have to do, several times a day (and often I'm so pleased they're doing it that I don't care where it happens), must be done in the garden. When I open the door to let them out in wet weather they stand looking at me with incredulity – didn't I know that dachshunds never go out in the rain? But if push comes to shove, a quick leak in one of the garden sheds is acceptable. A point in favour of these small German

Daisy, dachshund

dogs, with more than a hint of terrier: they detest getting wet so much that our borders are mostly no-go areas.

'We can't have male dogs because they lift their legs on my vegetables,' I hear. Quite. But bitches make yellow patches on the lawn. And in the 1960s and 1970s heyday of dwarf conifers, a spurt of urine could cause permanent damage to a prize specimen. Enthusiastic, cat-chasing dogs with a sporting look in their eye, lolloping labradors and retrievers, and ditzy King Charles spaniels that rush in all directions without thinking – none of these breeds is garden friendly.

What you need is a male dog with very short legs. However valiantly he lifts his leg, it always misses. Not a squirt but a sprinkle. That's what you want near your choice evergreens. I did have a lovely peke called Boozle, who, although challenged in the leg department, wasn't quite so suitable. With his splendid thick coat he was always doing it in his trousers and needed a lot of baths. This reminds me of a friend's cousin's aunt, who was stuck on a yacht where the lavatory didn't work, and she had to do it in a carrier bag and throw it overboard.

No, your ideal garden dog is a male dachshund – but of course if you haven't got a lawn, like me, a female is just as good.

Fashion

As they get older people seem to get stuck with a particular hairstyle. Whichever stylist does my hair I invariably end up with a 1960s Cilla Black look – that's if I don't get the softly curly Nancy Reagan, or the ubiquitous *à la grandmère*, with every curl betraying its roller-friendly origins. (The only alternative, which hairdressers are always recommending, is the 'choppy' look, in which I end up with lots of sticky-up bits going in every direction – said to make the recipient look younger.)

Perhaps purple plum trees are to gardens what the *à la grandmère* is to hairstyles. Sometimes, driving down suburban streets, you can imagine when the houses were just built, in the 1930s or 1940s, and how the owners, in line with neighbourhood choice, decided on the plum, together with laburnum, cherry and privet hedge, plus the single row of standard roses leading to the front door. I have particularly got it in for the purple plum tree, as its leaves never look entirely happy, and its general demeanour is always too dark for our Irish light – try taking a photograph that includes one and you'll notice that it makes a black hole in the view.

Bad hair day – the twisted hazel, *Corylus avellana* 'Contorta'

Variegated plants

How could I forget a love affair that lasted for at least thirty years? When we first came to Ireland, I remember an admired gardener of the old school saying rather acidly that all I wanted was the fancy stuff. At that stage I was drawn irresistibly towards oddities – the dwarf cultivar, the one with double flowers. Gaudy, multi-coloured leaves were what I wanted. Not that I'd ignore leaves of gold or purple: to me there was nothing more desirable than a bit of flash. Plain, honest green was not for me. How could such a passion cool to near indifference? But that's exactly what happened in my long association with variegated plants. I suppose it's a sort of growing up, my wanting the original green plant just as Nature made it, without any of the hectic patterns, stripes and streaks, mottling or spotting which so often suggest an attack of virus (although I understand that variegation has various causes).

Having condemned variegated plants, I'd like to now list a few exceptions – the plants I still love. With the proviso that you can always over-egg the pudding and spread too many variegated plants around, just a few, thoughtfully placed, can light up gardens in places such as Dublin. In places with higher light intensity and hotter summers than us the foliage of variegated plants can burn up.

I love *Miscanthus sinensis* 'Cosmopolitan' (1.8m/6ft). It has such crisp variegation, and very late flowers in November, when it looks good in a prominent corner spot at the beginning of the blue border. The moment the wispy leaves start falling off in winter and the clump looks untidy, we use sharp scissors to clean the stems completely of frizzled leaves. The seedheads make a great contribution to the garden picture right through until March. We have a lovely, striped form of the giant reed (*Arundo donax*, 4m/12ft), which is definitely more tender than the species (probably around Z9). I'm not certain exactly which variegated cultivar it is (it came from Holland), but it has brilliant, clean variegation. I think it (and the species itself, which is happy outdoors all year) looks better if the older stems are cut off in late spring as the young ones appear.

Midsummer, garden in rain. *Luma apiculata* 'Glanleam Gold' (an Irish cultivar) to the left – I wish I'd planted the green species instead. Top left, *Cornus mas* 'Variegata'.

Cornus mas 'Variegata' (6m/20ft) is the variegated form of the cornelian cherry, so called because the fruits are just like the translucent red stone called cornelian (I think it's also known as chalcedony) that we used to find on beaches in Scotland, along with rose quartz, amethyst quartz, moss agate and occasionally small garnets. The variegated leaves of this European and West Asian dogwood never assume a tired August look and remain fresh looking right through until autumn.

The twining evergreen Chinese climber *Trachelospermum jasminoides* 'Variegatum' is listed as zone 9 but here has never been affected by frost. The glossy leaves are cream and pale green, sometimes prettily flushed pink, and the fragrant, creamy flowers appear in July and August. This has now climbed its way to the top of the stone, south-east-facing wall of the mews, where it is forming a mutually beneficial entanglement with the lipstick-pink flowers of *Salvia involucrata* 'Bethellii' (1.5m/5ft), the salvia enjoying winter protection from the trachelospermum. Near by grow the rose we call 'Bengal Crimson' and rose 'Rhapsody in Blue', both putting on a mass of new buds in August.

Anyway, I always know when it's August just by looking at the stone of the terrace, which is scattered with clouds of creamy petals floating down from a small Chilean tree, *Luma apiculata* 'Glanleam Gold' (6m/20ft), which grows on the south wall of the house and is now alight with flowers. This variegated form, which originated on Valentia Island in Ireland, was given to me in the late 1970s, at the height of my passion for novelties. I now wish I'd planted the ordinary dark green species instead. However, the light-coloured leaves of 'Glanleam Gold' couldn't be better as a foil for the deep, dark black-purple flowers of *Clematis* 'Romantika'.

I will never forget one of the many succinct observations of Graham Stuart Thomas. He pointed out that many plants from the southern hemisphere have foliage that is slightly dead looking, when you compare it to the fresh green of plants from the northern hemisphere. The more I looked at my bulky specimen of corokia, or wire-netting bush, with his words resounding in my ears, the more I went off it for that reason, until finally we removed it.

My specimen of *Azara microphylla* (8m/26ft) from New Zealand is variegated, but I think Graham's opinion still applies. When viewed from a distance it always seems a slightly grubby yellow. I sometimes think of replacing it with the ordinary green species, but then I recall the delicious early spring scent of the flowers. One plant I'm definitely not changing is the variegated, small-leaved cream and green ivy that decorates the arches at the far end of the canal.

Recently I've found myself looking with a critical eye at purple- and red-leaved plants. Especially in winter, plants such as red-leaved cordyline seem alien to Ireland – I don't want the tropical look in midwinter – so out came my plant, as did many flashy phormiums. In summer, though, plants with red foliage can be another matter. I adore my cannas and my purple sugar cane (*Saccharum officinarum* 'Pele's Smoke', 2m/7ft) and my beautiful purple-black elder (*Sambucus nigra* 'Eva', also known as 'Black Lace', 4m/12ft), and I still think *Rosa glauca* (2m/7ft, Z2, but needs shade in hotter climates), with its reddish leaves and bluish bloom ,is madly pretty.

No plants

Gardens aren't only for growing plants. A friend was telling me about his brother's garden. In it is a garage, three sheds, a space dug out for the foundations of a greenhouse, a motorbike standing on the garden table waiting to be mended and another in the middle of the lawn. My friend overheard his sister-in-law asking his brother what the motorbike, a Moto Guzzi, was doing in the middle of the lawn. His brother replied, 'But it's an Italian garden, isn't it?'

Lawn, privet, rose bed

I've often wondered why, in the suburbs of most cities, you see thriving examples of front gardens that consist of a lawn, a rose bed and a privet hedge. How have these early twentieth-century gardens survived, caught in the cage of collective memory, with no desire to escape and sing? In the horticultural press there are a million advertisements, all promoting different machines and tools, as if no gardening is real unless a huge amount of action is taking place – mowing, edging, scarifying, clipping, deadheading, raking, sweeping, digging, spraying, hacking and sawing. Most of these operations would be needed for maintenance of such a garden and I sometimes wonder if that isn't the whole point of the lawn, rose bed and privet hedge style: it allows a gardener to step outside on a Saturday morning and lose himself (it has to be a him) by becoming so preoccupied with the repetition of weekly gardening jobs that he forgets all the niggling small worries.

Perhaps another reason for the unlikely survival of such gardens is that the lawn is mowed, the roses pruned and hedge clipped simply because they are there, and the idea of digging it all up and developing a more relaxed style of garden has never actually occurred to a series of different owners.

Must have own space

'The queens of the tribe . . . noticeably tolerant of dry conditions and will thrive almost anywhere,' remarks Graham Stuart Thomas of the soft-shield fern (*Polystichum setiferum*, 50cm/20in). It's taken me many years to learn just how good the many different forms of this wonderfully easy-going fern are. Today, in early August, after the hottest weather for thirty years, our soil dust dry and the earth cracking in places, there they are, my *Polystichum setiferum* Divisilobum Group 'Gracillimum' (formerly 'Green Lace') and 'Pulcherrimum Bevis', all under the big Bramley apple, all bright green and flourishing.

Fern names are excruciatingly complicated and I can't look at any of these ferns without thinking of slow nineteenth-century afternoons when there was nothing to do between lunch and tea except hunt for peculiar forms of native ferns and then bestow on them convoluted names such as 'Plumosodensum' – which turns out, on closer examination of the *RHS Plant Finder*, to have metamorphosed into 'Plumosomultilobum'. I daresay that at this very moment in some dusty office of taxonomy a young botanist is gathering the different fern names and re-sorting them according to his research, thus swiping the botanist who last renamed them in the eye.

The whole point of a fern is to be able to delight in its singular beauty, the intricacies of its design and the graceful way the fronds unfurl in spring. So a collection of thirty or so different ferns, all growing together in the same bed like a box of fancy cakes with multi-coloured icing, doesn't make sense to me. I've now reached the maximum number of ferns to which I can give positions that both justify their beauty of form and satisfy their growth requirements. Ideally, for a singleton fern, you need a shady spot in a corner or beside a path, so that you can stop and examine it intimately.

It was a sin the way I used to treat the majestic fern *Dryopteris wallichiana*. I grew it crammed up beside the statue at the end of the garden, so that the beautiful silhouette of the 1.2m/4ft fronds, which formed an immaculate shape of a tall vase, was destroyed. I finally had the courage to dig it up, divide it into five segments and replant them in a shady patch in the front garden.

Although spring is the time recommended for dividing ferns, I don't think new divisions like sitting around in cold soil. I've just – in early August, after heavy rain – divided a thirty-year-old

Matteuccia struthiopteris doesn't like conditions that are too dry.

clump of *Polystichum setiferum* Divisilobum Group, even though I asked several knowledgeable people when they thought I should divide it and they all considered I should wait until spring. My theory is that dividing in August gives the fern about twelve more weeks of warm soil for the roots to settle. Incidentally, some ferns, adiantum or maidenhair fern in particular, greatly resent being planted deeper than they were originally and the first time I divided the small, easy, maidenhair fern *Adiantum venustum* (20cm/8in), I killed most of the divisions. Some of the adiantums have exquisite coral-pink young fronds – for instance, the beautiful *A. aleuticum* 'Japonicum' (45cm/18in) given to me by plant collector Gary Dunlop from his garden in County Down, Northern Ireland.

My only long-term house plant is the ice-blue fronded rabbit's foot fern (*Polypodium aureum*, now *Phlebodium aureum*, 90cm/3ft), '*aureum*' because the ripe spores on the back of the leaves appear golden). This is one of those curious plants that actually prefers life in the drawing room to the humid comforts of the greenhouse. My plant receives a pint of water once a week in winter and twice a week in summer. The late Betty Farquhar, who lived at Ardsallagh, County Tipperary, and was not only a superb gardener but also had brilliant taste, had a pair of pots of this fern in her drawing room, where the pale blue of the fronds beautifully juxtaposed with the sheen of her violet-grey wild silk wallpaper.

This fern is easy to grow from spores, as follows: fill a small pot with peat-based potting compost; pour over a kettle of boiling water and allow to drain; cool for a minute or two and then shake over a frond which has ripe spores (very fine dust falling from the leaves); cover immediately with a polythene bag and seal; place in a cool, sunless room; after some weeks (or months) a green, velvety film will form on the surface of the pot, from which (an early stage of the growth of a fern) minute fronds will appear; when the tiny plants are big enough, separate and pot individually.

The most unusual fern here, *Athyrium filix-femina* 'Caput-Medusae' (35cm/15in), was a present from David Shackleton. This looks like parsley, with exceedingly congested, very frilly fronds. It's far more parsley-like than the parsley fern (cryptogramma) itself – indeed so convincing that people take no notice of it. So much for one of the rarest plants in the garden.

Angel's fishing rods

If you really want to torment someone who lives in a cold area – say anywhere in Continental Europe or below zone 8 in the USA – just mention the dierama or angel's fishing rod. Read no further if you live in such a place. You could, of course, insist that you'll grow it in pots in the greenhouse, but this doesn't work well: dieramas come from the Drakensburg Mountains, a comparatively cool area of South Africa. The sword-like leaves are evergreen and they need to be kept growing all winter, but they don't like warm greenhouses, coming as they do from airy, grassy mountainsides. You can't win.

The other essentials for growing dieramas are an isolated position in full sun with masses of light surrounding the plant, moisture in the growing season and good drainage in winter. Angel's fishing rods have been photographed too many times looking beautiful leaning over garden pools, giving the illusion that they are waterside or bog plants, which they most definitely are not.

You cannot squash a dierama into a crowded border, for much of the irresistible appeal of this iris relation is the slender flower stems, which form graceful arcs of perpetual motion, swinging backwards and forwards, the bell-like flowers suspended from pedicels fine as a mouse's eyelash. When seed is set, the stems bow low with the extra weight, but all winter the ballet continues, as they rise and fall, this way and that, quivering and shimmering, through until spring. Then the plants look untidy, and we cut the dead leaves carefully away with scissors, but occasionally we lose patience and chop the whole lot down, to no obvious bad effect. However, I think that long term this treatment would weaken the plants.

The succession of flowers begins with *Dierama pauciflorum* (60cm/24in) in late May. The plant we have has mauve-blue flowers and plenty of them, despite the specific epithet *pauciflorum*, meaning 'few-flowered'. The small, delicate dieramas follow on in June, with coral and very pale pink flowers, and then in July and August comes the tallest, *Dierama pulcherrimum*, in colours that include marshmallow pink, mid-pink and dark purple. There are many cultivars under the name 'Blackbird' – whether they have a right to it or not. I think all dieramas are heavenly plants; I adore them all, the bigger the better.

People who haven't seen angel's fishing rods before often think they're flowering grasses. Here they are growing with *Catananche caerulea*.

Self-sown seedlings, which take some years to flower, appear all round the parent plants. I find that if you have a small coral-flowered plant, you'll have similar seedlings; and tall pink flowers, ditto. Division is a worrying operation: the corms are jammed tightly together and on top of each other, and easily damaged when pulled apart. Underneath the corms you'll notice a few fat white roots, as well as stringy older ones. If you can manage to pot up sections with several corms plus an undamaged white root, so much the better. Keep them in a cool, airy greenhouse until established.

Agapanthus

My taste in agapanthus has veered from double agapanthus (shy to flower), through variegated cultivars (sulky growers) and desirable *A. inapertus* (75cm/30in; erratic bloomers) to a good white, still extant. But what I really want are the great big beautiful blue ones, the only plants that capture the essential beauty of these sumptuous late-summer South African plants, the very same ones that my grandfather grew, in a series of large containers, on the wide sandstone terrace of Broome House in Worcestershire, where the sun always seemed to shine.

Of course I have gorgeous deep, dark purples and the scarce, small, late-blooming white-flowered Irish cultivar 'Lady Moore', and also some neat self-sown seedlings in mid-blue, with low foliage, so the flowers are nicely displayed. But agapanthus seedlings are just like puppies: they are all good and you want to keep the lot.

As a general rule, the large-flowered cultivars with wide evergreen leaves are more tender than the narrow-leaved deciduous agapanthus. *The New Royal Horticultural Society Dictionary of Gardening* mentions that they thrive when overcrowded. I don't agree, and find the cycle of flowering goes thus: first year, settling in, few flowers; second year, decent amount of flowers; third year, a terrific show; fourth year, flowering diminished; fifth year, yet fewer flowers. The next step is compulsory division, best attempted in spring – an unforgettably tough job, involving brute strength, your best kitchen knife, a sharp spade and a hard surface on which to cut through the congested roots. I cut away lots of these: as they're damaged anyway, my reasoning is that there seems no point in replanting a great ball of dry and tangled roots. Position the divisions about 30cm/12in apart.

Agapanthus in containers need a rich, soil-based mixture. Regular applications of liquid fertilizer during summer until the buds form should encourage flowers. In the border, if I notice in autumn that the roots of long-established clumps are too near the surface, I throw a whole bucket (13.5 litres/3 gallons) of garden compost on top, with some soil on top of that to stop the birds pulling at it, thus applying a mulch and feed at the same time. I do this to many herbaceous plants that I'm putting off dividing. Another delaying tactic (I learned this from Nigel Marshall,

An elegant low-growing seedling agapanthus that turned up here.

head gardener for many years at Mount Stewart) is to chop off half the clump, remove some of the old soil and fill up the hole with garden compost plus fresh soil.

I've left until last the essential point of agapanthus growing: they must have a first-class position in full sun, just like two more native plants of South Africa, dieramas and kniphofias, both of which are equally insistent on sun, air and space.

As light as air

I've come to a conclusion as to why some of the prettiest plants are not more widely grown. I can imagine the meeting at a large nursery as the annual catalogue is being put together, with directors of the nursery, the photographer and a couple of designers looking on. The issue is whether to give picture space to *Gillenia trifoliata* or the latest hemerocallis or day lily. The gillenia (1.2m/4ft, Z4) grows wild in North America and is a very easy long-lived plant, happy in sun or part shade, which you shouldn't ever divide, and although said to prefer lime-free soil it is perfectly fine in this limey garden. The new day lily shows few signs of its original wild parents and owes much to the input of plant breeders. How can you expect the ethereal beauty of the gillenia, with its clouds of airy little white flowers with persistent red calyces on wiry stems, to compete with a true Jordan of the plant world, a high-glamour day lily with bright red velvet ruffles for petals and an inbuilt pout?

You rarely see a photograph of *Aster divaricatus* (60cm/24in). Each flower is a plain Jane of a small white daisy. Individually that is. But put together a cloud of little white daisies, notice that the tip of each petal is faintly splashed with mauve-crimson, and the colour is reflected in the centre of the flower. The branching, wiry stems are shiny black purple. Add the facts that the leaves never look tired in the hottest, dustiest summer, the flowers last for months, and – the best bit – this eastern USA aster will thrive in dry shade with never a hint of stress. My plants flowered every autumn in the same spot for twenty years. Finally we divided them when we redid the front garden and wanted lots of tiny daisies to flop over the edge of the paving.

Verbena bonariensis (2m/7ft), one of the darlings of recent years, is unbeaten as the queen of plants for making a luminous violet gauzy screen. That a plant of such delicacy should be able to compete with the stars is probably because it has a self-generating fan club – once seen, always wanted. I find it quite short-lived, but masses of seedlings appear each June.

I love all gypsophilas, for their airy, misty masses of white blossom, and I can't see them without thinking of cut-glass Waterford vases and sweet peas, shining dining-room tables, silver, round lace tablemats, colliding scents of flowers, furniture polish and roast potatoes, and everybody on their best behaviour. *Gypsophila* 'Rosenschleier' (45cm/18in) is easy to keep on a

Euphorbia corollata will root from basal cuttings in the spring.

raised bed where sun, good drainage and an open position are available, unlike the taller cultivars, which are inclined to succumb to competition in the borders. I have occasionally rooted stem cuttings of 'Rosenschleier' in the sand bed in the alpine house.

I'm not surprised if you don't know *Crambe filiformis* (60cm/24in). I'm always losing it – and I'm still not certain whether it's an annual or a short-lived perennial. When doing well it's a dreamy plant with thousands of tiny white cruciform flowers. It never seems to have enough leaves to keep it going, and the little foliage that there is, is rapidly mutilated by slugs. I have had several over the years, and just when the last one has gone, another will miraculously turn up from seed – but only the one, mind. A crambe that came originally from Beth Chatto as *Crambe koktebelica* (1.5m/5ft) is a wonderful plant because it's altogether smaller than *C. cordifolia* (2m/7ft), therefore with less obtrusive slug-eaten dull green leaves. I've nearly lost it a few times but managed to get root cuttings going at the eleventh hour. These cabbage relations absolutely insist on good sun, all day.

Euphorbia corollata (90cm/3ft) is a special favourite, which mimics gypsophila in its airiness, and I don't see why everybody doesn't grow this quietly beautiful American native. It doesn't set seed with me, so I occasionally root cuttings. I grow it on the sunny raised bed, where it blooms for a long season in late summer.

Mobile plants

When I try to analyse the difference between how I used to garden in the 1960s and 1970s compared to the present day, it seems to me that now a lot depends on how mobile a plant is. In those days popular plants were shrubs, dwarf conifers and heathers – plants that behaved themselves and stayed put. Even thinking about shrubs brings damp dark places to mind, underneath crowded rhododendrons collecting leafmould in Scotland where I grew up, with the cold drip-drip of water down the back of my scratchy Shetland jersey. When the big raindrops fell on the rhododendron leaves, each leaf gave a quick little bow towards the earth so that the water rolled off, but the stiff branches remained quite still.

Now, just think of a field of wheat in spring, the green shoots only inches high as the wind shimmers through them in waves of light, sweeping over the field in rippling curves.

Phormium on the move

Grasses and bamboos, the movers and shakers of the plant world, are much admired at the moment, and just looking out of the window I can see why: so much perpetual motion – a tumbling fountain of miscanthus, trembling stems of dierama, and so many plants that swing with the wind and sway with the breeze, with the grass *Molinia caerulea* subsp. *arundinacea* 'Transparent' (1.2m/4ft) presenting an airy display, stems and seedheads glittering to the sun and

The small paved area is easy to garden, and consists mainly of self-sown plants.

the ever-waving tall wands of *Arundo donax* (4m/12ft), the giant reed.

The gardens I most admire have loose planting, reminding me of the edges of fields and hedgerows. We were taught to plant in groups of three, five or seven – resulting in a series of blobs. But now I want to plant in long, flowing wavy lines: I want not only the plant to move but the planting itself to undulate along, all the time giving a suggestion of movement.

I must tell you about the coyote willow (*Salix exigua*, 8m/26ft). The slender leaves are pale green early in the season, but by August are at their silvery best. As these small, suckering trees are stooled (cut to about 90cm/3ft) every spring, the annual shoots are soft and flexible, constantly on the move, each fluttery leaf throwing light from a different angle. We always need good August performers and this is one of the best.

Church of the people

Garden centres provide the most innocent of amenities. They are not exactly a visit to your therapist, not quite a church, nor a park, a pub or a restaurant, and yet there may be peace enough to think, plants enough to calm you, fresh air and a walk in a safe place. You can sit down and have a big lunch, your children can play in safety, you can buy supplies for your dog. You can have a long discussion with a complete stranger on the shape, form, colour, hardiness, care, feeding, price and estimated height of an unusual plant; you can contemplate trays of colourful bedding plants, and keep changing your mind about which to buy, and of course you'll be returning next Saturday for

Lilium regale

an update on new arrivals and to continue your ongoing pursuit of planting partners. There are few opportunities for such pleasant conversation, so free of other agendas. It is sort of an extension of the conversation that takes place a thousand times a day about the weather, in which there is no necessity for either party to reveal anything whatsoever about themselves – a simple and curiously satisfying form of social interaction.

Winter skeletons

Nobody is in two minds about teasels. While I love their brutish prickly presence, uncompromising attitude and swaggery stance, Val hates them. A row about teasels starts once a week, the teasel being the plant more than any other that causes garden arguments.

Val doesn't like their pushy manners, the way they jab neighbouring plump pink roses and velvet foxgloves, and the arrogant way they insert themselves into prime positions, with a true developer's mindset concerning occupation of space.

I love the teasels' winter silhouettes, viewed against the sun, their stems and seedheads gaunt and dry, all the threat gone out of them. The biennial teasel is a mighty producer of seed, so you must remove 99 per cent of the seedlings. As the garden faces south-west, every autumn I move seedlings for the following year and plant them in a staggered line leading towards the south, so that we see the stems backlit by the sun as we follow the path from the house. Another delight of owning teasels in winter is when you hear excited twittering and out of the corner of your eye see flashes of red and yellow as flocks of goldfinches descend, hungry for seed.

Midsummer teasels are a study in tall, spiny grey-green elegance, the pale lilac flowers opening in a peculiar way, from the middle to the ends of the bristly, egg-shaped flowerheads. The leaves on either side of the stem meet in the middle, forming decorative cups. These hold water after summer rain, but I can never understand how this collected water, which acts as a death trap for small thirsty insects, is of benefit to the plant.

The common teasel (*Dipsacus fullonum*, 2m/7ft) is very similar to *D. sativus*. The hooked bracts of the latter are used for raising the nap on cloth. Apparently the inspiration for the inventor of Velcro was when he saw the prickly teasel seedheads locked in spiny embrace. Incidentally, teasel seedlings are very deceptive: when I saw them first I thought they were big, healthy primula plants – except they had spines.

All is not lost if you don't at first position your teasels to catch the sun. Just pull out the tall dried stem in one piece, choose the appropriate position, dig a spade's-depth hole, shove the base into the hole and then replant, heeling it in, as they say. This means to make the soil very firm by pressing down hard with the heel end of your boot. Exactly the same action is used for firming soil around just-planted bare-root trees. You can do the same with the decorative, long-lasting dried globular seedheads of *Allium cristophii* (50cm/20in). Odd singleton seedheads can be rounded up to form a big grouping where none was before. Nobody will guess.

The spent seedhead of giant fennel (*Ferula communis*, 2.5m/8ft, Z8), a great tall umbellifer, forms a beautiful skeleton, exciting from any angle. The dried flowers on tall stems of *Miscanthus sinensis* var. *condensatus* 'Cosmopolitan' (2m/7ft), once the withered foliage is tidied up, form a lovely winter picture; another good grass is *Calamagrostis* x *acutiflora* 'Karl Foerster' (1.5m/5ft). The dried stems and seedheads of *Sedum spectabile* (45cm/18in) and *Phlomis russeliana* (90cm/3ft) cynara, echinops and astilbe are also satisfying.

Seedheads of *Ferula communis* subsp. *glauca*

Eryngiums

To start at the end rather than the beginning, the first thing you need to know about eryngiums or sea hollies, or at any rate the European species (excluding the ubiquitous Miss Willmott's ghost, *E. giganteum*, 90cm/3ft, which is a mad self-sower) is how to propagate them. I'm always having to transplant eryngiums, because what initially appears to be an ideal spot – full sun, masses of air, perfect drainage – turns out to be quite the reverse when some great Schwarzenegger of a plant, or at least a plant that's been doing some long-term intense body building, moves in and takes the light away. Of course this is nothing whatsoever to do with my bad judgement about the choice of position in the first place.

Eryngiums, as you will have read in books, resent disturbance. Indeed they are often so resentful about it that they die. But if you manage to dig up a long piece of the succulent root, and hold it in your hand the right way up all the way to the potting shed so that you don't forget, and then chop the root, using a sharp knife, into sections about 5cm/2in long, using a straight cut at the top and an angled cut at the bottom (otherwise you'll get muddled again before they go into the pot), push the sections into the mixture angle-side down, very lightly cover the top and leave the pot for many months in a cold greenhouse or frame, you'll have the deep satisfaction of noticing a faint green on the surface of the cutting mix, which very slowly develops into baby eryngiums. I've done this regularly with *E.* x *zabellii* 'Violetta' (45cm/18in), *E.* x *oliverianum* (45cm/18in, Z5) and *E. amethystinum* (60–90cm/2–3ft).

Were I to describe just how lovely the thistle-like flowers are of these prickly members of the *Apiaceae* (formerly *Umbelliferae*) or what I think of as the cow parsley or Queen Anne's lace family, I would definitely run out of all the shiny adjectives such as silvery and sparkly, and every word for colour, provided it's blue, or violet, or a mixture of both and possibly a million other ways to bring pictures of blue into your head, with sea and sky and sapphire and lapis lazuli and all that stuff. Visitors mention for the whole of July and August how much they like my 'thistles'.

I've had this sea holly so long I'm not certain of the name, but I believe it's *Eryngium* x *oliverianum*.

I understand that the European *Eryngium maritimum* (60cm/24in) is naturalized on the east coast of the USA. Despite it being native to Ireland (as well as Britain), I don't find this species all that easy. Not surprising, considering it wants to live on a nice sandy beach, sunning itself all day, occasionally being photographed by passing botanists. Drainage is obviously the key word here. I suppose the most irresistible individual flower is found in *E. alpinum* (60cm/24in; easy but slow from seed), quickly recognized because the prickly-looking flowers are kitten-soft to touch, but this species from high European meadows is not long in flower compared to *E. oliverianum*, for example. I've grown North African *E. variifolium* (60cm/24in) for many years (you can divide this one easily) and it's not the most glamorous, but the small flowers and bracts make a pleasing silvery green picture en masse. I gather *E. planum* 'Blaukappe' (60cm/24in) was originally bred for the cut flower market. The main flower in the middle is encircled by more tiny flowers. It is long lasting in the garden and well deserving of a top sunny place – and yet another customer I've had to propagate by root cuttings in order to relocate it.

Pyrenean *E. bourgatii* (30cm/12in) is a cracking small plant that has been growing here since the early 1980s. Long lived, and a regular supplier of exactly the amount of seedlings I want, this front-of-border treasure invites comments on its conspicuously silver variegated leaves from May onwards. 'Oxford Blue' is an excellent cultivar, but they're all good. The stems of the flowers are washed in liquid violet.

Most of the eryngiums from the USA, Mexico and South America look quite different, almost as if they're bromeliads and related to pineapples. To me, *E. pandanifolium* (2.5m/8ft) is a gem, albeit a very large prickly one, best never approached – weeding anywhere near it requires thick leather gloves. The large clusters of tiny purple-green flowers arrive in autumn, but I grow it for the foliage; in the form I grow this is the blue of the egg of a duck, which reminds me of some of the amazing plants at Sean Hogan's Cistus Nursery in Portland, where there's a much lower rainfall than in Ireland and glaucous foliage looks twenty times bluer than it does here because of the sun and dryness. Rather than divide *E. pandanifolium* – anybody who has will know how bloody this operation can be – I just chop a bit off when it gets too big. All beginners will fall for *E. proteiflorum* (90cm/3ft), of which you will see ravishing pictures in catalogues. With me this produced one gorgeous silver flower in cold November and immediately died.

Araliaceae

Shopping centres have a strange effect on me. I go only on wet Saturday mornings and only to visit Marks and Spencer and escape as fast as possible. But the moment I enter the central mall, it seems that the warm stuffy air seduces me into asking myself: 'Why don't I just buy that handbag right now? I can always throw it away if it doesn't suit.'

Somehow this attitude has crept over the wall into garden centres. Somehow plants have become expendable and replaceable. The Victorians planted trees and imagined their descendants growing old in the shade of mature woodlands. They had confidence in a future. But, blasphemous as it sounds, I now think of some trees as temporary. I want them to strut their stuff to please me right now, and if they don't look good, bye-bye.

Now we get into the more sensitive area of which trees I'd put into this category. Equal first choice are trees that sucker (I've no hesitation in cutting away a whole trunk of *Aralia elata* (14m/30ft) and trees that you can stool, such as *Paulownia tomentosa* (20m/65ft), *Rhus typhina* (10m/33ft) and *Ailanthus altissima* (30m/100ft). This last is a bad weed in warmer climates but well behaved here, with super-large feathery leaves.

I'm drawn towards the *Araliaceae* family. I find its members easy to grow and fascinating in their diversity. I believe that they tolerate the soil here, which, although it looks dark and rich when wet, has had too much expected of it as it's been gardened since the house was built in 1830. It could be that there's been a divorce between farming and gardening, and gardeners are no longer concentrating enough on leaving the soil fallow and giving it a rest, but, like most gardeners, I can't afford to leave big empty spaces. So I'm trying to grow easily satisfied plants instead: those which like a perpetual diet of lean cuisine. The aralia family includes ivy, which will take the toughest conditions, while many of the most exciting members come from New Zealand, where the soil is nutrient-low.

Carmel Duignan, who has an inspiring garden just down the coast from here, fired my interest in pseudopanax, which make very good small, slow-growing evergreen trees for sheltered gardens. At first sight *Pseudopanax crassifolius* (5m/16ft) is a very odd plant. *P. ferox* is even odder and a bit more tender. The extraordinary-looking juvenile foliage of both these strange New Zealanders is narrow and elongated, giving an effect like a dead umbrella, with just the spokes left. *P. ferox* has more toothed juvenile leaves than *P. crassifolius* and can take very dry conditions, making a good long-term pot plant. I pop mine, still in its pot, inside another pot a tiny bit bigger sunk in the soil; in autumn I lift it out and move it to a sheltered position near the potting shed so that I can drag it inside if cold weather threatens. Apparently the juvenile leaves of these two species evolved in such a way in order to appear unpalatable to giant grazing birds, now extinct. Once the plants grow tall enough to escape the threat of passing beaks a metamorphosis takes place and the leaves turn from ugly ducklings into swans, becoming much shorter and more like typical, evergreen leaves. Both these intriguing and peculiar-looking small trees look best in groups rather than as singletons. The foliage of the next four pseudopanax is the same from the beginning. 'Adiantifolius' (3m/10ft) is a small evergreen tree with large shiny leaves shaped like those of a maidenhair fern. 'Sabre', 'Trident' and 'Gold Splash' are all excellent too. But I like pseudopanax so much that I'd try any.

The celebrity of the aralia family has to be *Schefflera taiwaniana* (6m/20ft), discovered by Bleddyn and Sue Wynn-Jones, which made its debut at the Chelsea Flower Show in 2005. This tropical-looking tree, with dark evergreen long-fingered leaves, looks as though it should be living in the foyer of an office block rather than outside during a Dublin winter. Twice last year I panicked in cold weather and went out at night and covered it in fleece. I'm delighted to say it survived.

A note about design: when I planted the group of *Aralia elata* (around nine to begin with) in the gravel garden, it had a dramatic effect within minutes. The trees, already 3m/10ft high, immediately changed the scale. Suddenly I was standing in the middle of a small copse. It presents a new angle on an old garden to introduce a group of small trees, and to be able to walk among them on gravel rather than mud, all in one afternoon. Try it. In winter these aralias are like so many long walking sticks, but in summer they each open their green parasol of leaves and cast interesting shadows on the gravel. Incidentally, I didn't realize until I laid it that gravel is considerably brighter and lighter to look at than the green of a grass lawn, which seems to absorb rather than reflect light. My trees were cheap: they're just the plain species as opposed to the said-to-be-desirable, slow and expensive variegated form.

I want this particular space to be quite different from the remainder of the garden. When you are in it, I want you to feel far removed from the typical Irish or English flower-garden look. The more alien-looking the plants the better. There's a decent large banana (although it only recovers from winter by the end of June), many hedychiums or ginger lilies, a palm and several bamboos. The exotic noises and strange rustlings that the leaves of these plants make bring to mind a line by Tennessee Williams: 'Wonderful sounds, the palms and banana trees make, like ladies running barefooted in silk skirts downstairs.'

Pseudopanax ferox, not as hardy as *P. crassifolius*, seems happy kept long-term as a pot plant.

Hardy orchids

Land where wild orchids grow is somehow blessed. I feel honoured when they occasionally turn up, where the soil is undisturbed. Native or otherwise, hardy orchids are thrilling plants, especially in early summer, when the queen of lady's slipper orchids, North American *Cypripedium reginae* (60cm/24in), produces its mottled pink and white bosomy flowers surrounded by undulating light green leaves. I once had a clump with twenty-seven blooms, but by dividing it at the wrong time of year, in midsummer, I killed the lot. To stop the stems toppling over when I replanted it, I pushed it too deeply into the soil, thus causing terminal rot. It's essential that the growing shoot should be at soil level, and if you buy one of these expensive plants in a pot, when you plant it make sure you keep the level of the growing shoot and the soil level exactly the same as they were in the pot.

One way of keeping the plant firmly in the ground, without burying the tuber, is to place big stones over the spreading roots, leaving the central snout clear. *Cypripedium calceolus* var. *pubescens* (50cm/20in), a widespread American and Japanese lady's slipper, grew well here for years. Then it became a victim of virus, with pinched growth and patchy green leaves, so I flung it out – as you should do with all virused plants, to protect other plants from infection. I now have a new plant from a different source.

Dactylorhizas (I grow what was given to me as *D.* x *braunii*, 30–45cm/12–18in) also won't tolerate deep planting – a fraction below the surface is the correct depth. Even to think of dividing these spotted-leaved wonders with light purple-speckled flowers makes me squirm. You can sense the way the fleshy roots detest being handled. You must ease them apart with the gentlest of squeezing and throw out the withered old tuber. Before the shock of daylight hits, replant them in a mix rich in humus – peaty will do, but leafmouldy is better. Early autumn is best for this operation, and even then next year's green shoot is obvious. Mark the position with several canes. Remember that the casual stamp of a garden boot means death.

Roscoeas will deceive you, because they look expensive, delicate and a bit like orchids. But in fact they are easy, unfussy about soil and happy in shade. Their rhizomatous roots are frost tender,

Dactylorhiza x *braunii* can be divided regularly. Be careful not to plant it too deeply.

and unlike the orchids above must be deeply planted, below the level of frost in your area. They don't appear above ground until June, so you must mark their position well. Lemon-yellow Chinese *Roscoea cautleyoides* (50cm/20in) and purple *R. humeana* (30cm/12in) have grown here for twenty-five years or more and we rarely divide them. Recently available is brilliant-red *R. purpurea* 'Red Gurkha'. What a star!

Potbound

Theoretically a container-grown plant is ideal. But what about a plant that was repotted only yesterday into a larger pot, so that the garden centre can charge more for it? The moment you turn it upside down everything falls away. I find that bits of compost, especially the barky bits, fall into my shoes. I clear up the mess, sigh my middle-aged sigh, and shove the remains into the ground regardless.

Potbound *Artemisia lactiflora*, the white mugwort (1.5m/5ft, Z4) needs surgery on congested roots before planting.

There is a moment with a plant in a container when the potting mix holds nicely, like a perfectly cooked soufflé – firm but soft, neither stiff nor collapsed. But very often, the plant has been in the pot too long, the roots have tied themselves into irretrievable knots and the poor thing is a picture of potbound misery.

Even with a good soak in a bucket of water prior to planting, the centre of the rootball can still be dry. The plant will be so jammed into its pot that you may have to cut away the pot using secateurs, if it's plastic, or even smash the pot if it's terracotta. I see no point in planting a constipated wodge of roots. If you cut away most of them, the plant has a better chance of developing fresh roots. Often when I dig up a sick-looking plant, the rootball is still in the shape of its original pot and the roots, trapped in dry peat, have never managed to escape into the surrounding soil.

I cut away a lot of the root of potbound ordinary herbaceous plants – asters, campanulas, doronicums, heleniums, phlox and so on – but only in the growing season. I wouldn't do so with a plant that dislikes root disturbance, or a plant with fleshy roots such as a peony or alstroemeria. I also cut away much of the root beforehand when potting up tender plants for overwintering in the greenhouse, such as pelargoniums and fuchsias.

Blue border

To begin with, the blue border existed mostly in my imagination: in reality it never looked quite blue enough. Sometimes people would say, when standing practically on top of it, 'Where is the blue border?' I suppose I've always been in love with blue flowers – perhaps not so much the flower, more the colour. This summer I even overheard myself saying 'growing my colours' – not a word about the plants. Just a slip of the tongue, you understand.

Irresistible to me are the blue of gentians growing in the melting snows of the Alps, the Madonna blue of Renaissance paintings, the ultramarine of cornflowers and the first heart-stopping sight of the blue Himalayan poppy. I adore all these colours, and always think the one I'm looking at is the best blue of all. But there aren't enough to satisfy my cravings: no blue roses, daffodils, dahlias or lilies. So mauves and lilacs and violets have crept into my blue border, and all the poor relations of blue, which I love just as much, such as the washy silver-mauve of my late-blooming *Aster ericoides* (1m/3ft), which seems so appropriate for the waning year.

If I could only take my own advice, perhaps my blue border would work more often. That advice would be to take a lot of one easy plant and run it through the whole bed, and then follow on through the summer with a succession of similarly reliable plants: *Geranium pratense* 'Mrs Kendall Clark' (60cm/2ft), *Anchusa azurea* (1.5m/5ft), lots of catmint (nepeta – not sure which cultivar mine is, as I've had it for so long, 60cm/24in), *Geranium* 'Rozanne' (45cm/18in), various aconitums, *Galega* x *hartlandii* 'Lady Wilson' (1.5m/5ft), *Campanula lactiflora* (1.5m/5ft), asters, perovskias, salvias and so on. In reality, the best moment in the border is probably when my royal blue cornflowers are at their peak, around midsummer, with the white foxgloves and the cherry pink poppies (don't ask me what these colours are doing here) and of course the delphiniums. These are unequalled in midsummer; no other plant has such miraculous presence, such celestial blue spires and such a tiresome list of requirements.

We sow cornflowers (*Centaurea cyanus*, height variable) in late autumn in seed trays. We put the trays into polythene bags and then into the airing cupboard for germination. Fresh seed comes up within ten days. The seedlings are pricked out into small pots and put in the greenhouse for

winter. By late March they need to be potted on into 1.5 litre/2½ pint pots. This may seem like work, but by early May I have decent plants to fill the huge space left where I have just taken out the tulips. L'Oréal (which I know a lot about as I'm a hair product junkie) would definitely say cornflowers are worth it. I made a mistake this year and grew a dwarf cultivar, which was horribly blobby and had mildew from an early stage. Never again. The tall cultivars, which require some staking, are what we want. We've also tried sowing love-in-a-mist (nigella) in pots this autumn to get decent plants for early next summer.

Some of our delphiniums have been here since the 1970s, when we bought them at Chelsea Flower Show from Blackmore and Langdon (a firm that has been hybridizing delphiniums since early last century). You have to start thinking about delphiniums in winter, because that's when the slugs are forming queues around the plants. Delphiniums themselves are greedy feeders; at the moment we're using pelleted chicken manure and mulching with garden compost. We don't thin out the shoots in spring as is sometimes recommended, but inspect our plants daily in the growing season and often adjust their staking. We constantly slosh them with water as they come into flower. The moment they go over (don't wait around for the very last flower to fade, or there won't

Cornflowers, delphiniums, opium poppies and seakale, with self-seeded foxgloves, in the blue border in June be enough summer left for them to re-bloom) chop the whole plant, leaves and all, to soil level. Feed lavishly and water regularly for more delphiniums in September.

Sometimes you hear people condemn *Campanula lactiflora* (1.5m/5ft) for being so ordinary. But that's what I love about it: it's easy to grow, easy on the pocket, easy on the eye – although it seeds around with vigour. I'd always heard of the cultivar 'Prichard's Variety', reputedly a good violet blue. So some years ago I bought it from several sources, and they were all different: some bluer than the others, some pale mauve. Curiously enough, as my photographer friend Diane Tomlinson mentioned, the pale colours show up best from a distance. I can see exactly what she means.

Aconitums (not much staking required) feature strongly in the border. *Aconitum* 'Stainless Steel' (1.2m/4ft) is the earliest, with long-lasting spires of light blue, much nicer in reality than in a photograph. *A.* x *cammarum* 'Bicolor' (white-edged blue), 'Bressingham Spire' (dark blue, very slender spikes) and the Irish cultivar 'Newry Blue' (navy blue) are also good. One of the best plants in the garden (I don't have the correct name for it) is a tall (3m/10ft) August-blooming aconitum with rich, deep blue flowers. Goodness knows where it came from, but I reckon it must have some of the climbing species in its parentage as the stems attempt to wind at the tips. This is so good that I now have it in four different places.

A nice, old-fashioned plant that we've grown for years is *Galega* x *hartlandii* 'Lady Wilson', (1.2m/4ft), which has lupin-like mauve and cream flowers. From the distance, in a mass, they form clouds of pale lilac. We were quite happy to keep deadheading the plants to prolong flowering, and I loved the flower colour, but I found that there is a huge amount of leafage. So this autumn we took out the lot, as I want a light and airy feel to the border, a see-through, filigree effect, and the galega's foliage was too overpowering. To make amends for its removal I've divided up my clump of *Phlox paniculata* (1.5m/5ft) – I think this is the species itself rather than one of its many cultivars. I've planted the divisions in a loose, winding drift and I'm looking forward to the luminous pale mauve flowers next August.

Just as the cornflowers run through the border giving a pointillist effect of bright blue, the Irish native *Knautia arvensis* (1.5m/5ft), a lovely quiet plant, dots the border with little puffs of pale blue scabious-like flowers for months in late summer. And, however common it is, I can never get enough of *Verbena bonariensis* (2m/7ft) and its minute violet flowers on tall thin stems. Every colour you put it with looks just right.

It was some time before it entered my head that blue foliage would add depth and texture to the blue border. Now a South African shrub, the honey flower (*Melianthus major*, 2m/7ft), is in several places and is a telling component for its beautiful glaucous blue leaves. (I never tire of this plant and always keep spares under glass in case of cold winters.) Another plant (in this case herbaceous) is the Irish native seakale (*Crambe maritima*, 90cm/3ft), which has, in the words of Graham Stuart Thomas, 'perhaps the most beautiful of all large glaucous leaves . . . the wide

Delphiniums, cornflowers, aconitums, pale mauve *Campanula lactiflora* and the first flowers of angel's fishing rods

blades exquisitely curved and lobed'. A huge cluster of small white honey-scented flowers appears in June.

I suppose it would be poor taste to line up one's friends and then classify them in the order of how much one liked them. Likewise with plants. Nevertheless, you can take it that I love all salvias, but certain salvias are absolutely tops. With star quality in the blue border is *Salvia guaranitica* (1.5m/5ft), which has thrived in the same spot for at least twenty-five years. *S. uliginosa* (2m/7ft) has sky-blue flowers and every year I remark to myself that I need more. I haven't quite hacked the way to keep it going – sometimes it lives through the winter outside, and sometimes even if I put it in a pot for winter in the greenhouse it dies. Still, for a gauzy blue veil in late summer, this plant is unbeatable.

Val had an idea that I'm hoping to try on a bigger scale next year – that of training *Clematis* x *durandii* (1.5m/5ft) upright to metal supports. For years this clematis, which has herbaceous *C. integrifolia* as one parent to explain its habit, ran about at ground level, draping nearby plants with deep violet blue flowers. This year, tied to a support, it bloomed at 1.2m/4ft in the air. Soon I hope to have many more groups of this beautiful blue along the front of the border, within reach of the canal for watering.

Red border

I used to think that my big epiphany about organizing colours took place in the early 1980s at Mount Stewart. The grand parterre, laid out in the 1920s on the south side of the house by Edith, Lady Londonderry, is planted on one side in pastel colours and on the other in hot colours. Suddenly all was clear. From that moment on I began to look at colours properly. No longer would I distribute the day's haul of plants from the garden centre in the first available spaces, as if dropped from a low-flying aeroplane.

But recently, as I looked out of the main windows here at the red border on the left and the blue on the right, I remembered a recurring picture I used to paint when I was at school. On the left-hand side everything would always be dark and cloudy, with angry red in the sky; to the right all was light and sunny. If you peered hard to the left, you'd notice grotesque faces hidden in the bark of the trees, but to the right there were houses with their windows open so that you could see into light-filled rooms. It was strange to find that I was doing the same picture again in the garden, although Mount Stewart no doubt stirred the memory.

I find colours both dazzling and maddening – my eyes can get almost drunk on a particular one, and I can think of none other. I've been shuffling the plants around in the red border for nearly three decades. At the beginning the border consisted mostly of several dwarf red berberis, which I now accuse of being the ultimate in blobbiness, and rose 'Marlena', a somewhat unpleasant red. One year I was mesmerized by scarlet – the English pillar-box type of red – such as that of *Lychnis chalcedonica*, 90cm/3ft) and *Crocosmia* 'Lucifer' (1.2m/4ft). Soon the balance had to be redressed by adding more of the blue red shades, such as crimson nicotianas and *Astrantia* 'Ruby Wedding' (80cm/32in). Then it was the turn of shocking pink, such as a 1960s lipstick-pink form of *Phygelius aequalis* (1.5m/5ft) and lots of annual deep pink cosmos for late summer.

I had a long affair with purple foliage. There were *Euphorbia amygdaloides* 'Rubra' and *E. dulcis* 'Chameleon' (45cm/18in, Z7) – both spoilt by mildew; *Heuchera micrantha* 'Plum Pudding' (30cm/12in) – mutilated by vine weevil; *Cercis canadensis* 'Forest Pansy' (3m/10ft, Z4) – succumbed to mysterious fungus; and several purple-leaved phormiums. I like purple phormiums

Heleniums, poppy seedheads and *Lilium henryi*, with tetrapanax in the background

in summer, but in Irish winters they seem inappropriately colourful and I'd rather grow them in pots so that I can move them in and out of view. The castor-oil plant (*Ricinus communis*, 1.5m/5ft) is absolutely out: not only is it dangerously poisonous, but I can't look at its shiny, fingered, deep red-purple leaves without thinking of poisoned umbrellas.

I still grow *Rosa glauca* (2m/6ft) and love it as much as ever for its soft pinky mauve leaves with a bluish waxy bloom and its airy silhouette. If you want the deepest black-purple lacy leaves, go for *Sambucus nigra* 'Eva' (3m/10ft), a super form of the wild elder. I have this in two places, but am thinking of removing one, because when I screw up my eyes and look at it from a distance, this shrub appears like a black hole or gap in the border – but of course I'll keep the other. *Persicaria microcephala* 'Red Dragon' was popular here for a time – the purple leaves are prettily marked with silver – but then we had a hot summer and it lost its manners and sprawled all over nearby plants. Blood will always out – this is, after all, a cousin of the giant knotweed. Until recently, *Knautia macedonica* (60cm/24in) decorated the front of the border with a non-stop display of little crimson pincushion flowers.

At the moment (this could change) I'm transfixed by the colour orange. Last autumn I heard an artist explain that orange was a much easier colour to cope with than red. I agree, but it has taken me years to come to that conclusion – orange can be a scary colour to begin with. Not only is *Lilium henryi* (1.5m/5ft), of which I'm very fond, easy to grow but also Augustine Henry (1857–1930), who discovered it in China growing near the Yangtze Gorge, used to live next door at 47 Sandford Road. A healthy group of his lovely lily does well in dryish shade within 3m/10ft of the party wall,

unfailingly producing light orange, pendulous, spotted Turk's-cap flowers in July.

Most crocosmias (montbretias) 'go back' or slowly deteriorate if you don't divide them regularly. I find that *Crocosmia masoniorum* 'Firebird' (1.2m/4ft) is an exception – this South African iris family member takes a few years to settle down again after division (as does *C.m.* 'Rowallane Yellow', 1.2m/4ft). 'Firebird' has glowing, vibrant deep orange flowers in August with a beautiful way of displaying its flowers, as if they are genuflecting towards you. Crocosmias, as well as other South Africans such as agapanthus, dieramas and kniphofias, insist on sun and moisture in the growing season. They all dislike being jostled by neighbouring plants.

Kniphofias, which for their colour (often flaming red and orange) should be in this border, are mostly growing elsewhere, in more open, sunny gravelled areas which suit them better. A scarce red hot poker here is *Kniphofia* 'Erecta' (1m/3ft) in which each little sparkling orange pendulous flower behaves oddly as it ages, turning upwards as if thrilled to be pollinated (I'm not certain that this means they have been pollinated – perhaps they're just old). I don't know of any other kniphofia that does this. Gary Dunlop, the nurseryman from County Down, informs me that *K.* 'Erecta' (90cm/3ft) is a sport or

The red border in August, with *Lythrum salicaria*, cannas, salmon pink Cactus dahlias, heleniums, eupatoriums and (leaning over the path), *Knautia macedonica*. I've taken a lot of this planting out now, but I've added more lythrum, which I love with water.

Crocosmia 'Star of the East' has especially large flowers.

hybrid of *K. uvaria* and was known to W.E. Gumbleton of Cork (1840–1911), the nineteenth-century horticulturist.

Another special poker is *K. thomsonii* var. *thomsonii* (formerly *K. thomsonii* var. *snowdenii* 90cm/3ft). This is very distinct, because the flowers are well separated from each other, making the outline of the flower spike quite different to any other. It is in bloom for most of summer, but Graham Stuart Thomas describes it as 'a rare and tender species only suitable for the mildest districts'.

Cirsium rivulare 'Atropurpureum' (1.2m/4ft), a sophisticated plant with purple thistles on willowy stems, used to languish in the doldrums of taste until it appeared at the Chelsea Flower Show, featuring prominently in the winning garden. This needs a position in the front of the border, as the leaves dislike competition and need full sunlight.

The more transient members of the red border's congregation include penstemons, verbenas salvias, cosmos and opium poppies. I mark with a stake any of the poppies with especially vibrant colours that I want to seed. *Hedysarum coronarium* (60cm/24in) is a plant I like, which despite my efforts is short-lived; the pea-like flowers are pretty soft crimson and nicely interspersed with bluish green clover-like foliage. I don't find it easy from seed, but have occasionally grown it from cuttings. (June Blake, who has a fascinating nursery close to her brother Jimi's garden in County Wicklow, sometimes has this. The dark purple-leaved cow parsley (*Anthriscus sylvestris* 'Ravenswing', 60cm/24in), self-seeds in just the right amount, providing a ferny dark background for red tulips and another pretty biennial, *Angelica sylvestris* 'Vicar's Mead' (90cm/3ft) has reddish leaves and umbels of pink-flushed flowers.

Tender plants, other than essential cannas and dahlias, include my much-loved *Salvia confertiflora* (1.5m/5ft), which has rough leaves and plush velvet orange-red flowers. Grown from cuttings, this doesn't bloom until August, but plants dug up in autumn and overwintered in the greenhouse flower much earlier. The Brazilian plume (*Justicia carnea*, 2m/6ft), a greenhouse evergreen with shiny purple foliage, is a new adventure for me as a bedding plant: cuttings are easy, and flower when young, growing to 90cm/3ft in year one, producing sticky flowers of a peculiar Germolene pink.

For years I've challenged anyone who dared to suggest that roses were unsuitable for this border. But every time I weeded this bed I got jabbed in the bum by a rose. So gradually, beginning with

'Alexander' (a sizzling vermilion) and 'Trumpeter' (a demanding red), I began to take them out. Some roses lost out on the blackspot front – 'Dusky Maiden' and 'Orange Triumph', for example. I loved the colour of both, but naked stems and spotty leaves won't do. I like 'Frensham', but it went too. And I love *Rosa* x *odorata* Sanguinea Group, which I wouldn't be without, despite a name that suggests odours and blood. (This plant originally came to me with the romantic name of 'Bengal Crimson'.) However, I dug up the other roses in the great clean sweep, the big garden upheaval that took place last autumn.

I am now growing alstroemerias in pots so I can plonk them about wherever extra colour is needed.

The catalyst for my digging up nearly all the red border was the sight of a piece of public planting at the side of a street in Metz, in northern France. It was unbelievably light and airy, a shimmer of green, white and silver, in a simple rectangular space. Distributed throughout the whole bed were many plants of the white form of potato flower, *Solanum laxum* 'Album' (climber). It is vigorous in habit, but there it had been trained to 90cm/3ft cylinders of nearly invisible wire. There were white salvias intermingling with a great mass of silvery green, extremely tactile pennisetums with some pale grey foliage, perhaps lamb's ears, perhaps artemisia. The whole effect was dreamy.

I arrived home, looked out of the window and didn't like what I saw: many years of adding plant after plant, applying layer upon layer of colour; like a painting that's been laboured over too long, the red border appeared heavy and overworked in places. There was too much dense mid-green foliage, such as that of dahlias and roses, and I'd overdone the eupatoriums (Joe Pye weed) and the heleniums. Even the knautias went from the front of the bed. Taking most of it out gave me an immediate sense of freedom, of release from pressure, and suddenly I had space to move – to reinvent, to plan anew.

I love the garden in all its moods; I love the air and the sky and all things green, my great calm in the middle of everything else. I never want to be a curator, just looking after areas of the garden made years ago; I want to be a creator, and reinvent all the time. I believe that neither gardens nor people can stand still. Change is everything.

Further reading

Cave, Yvonne and Valda Paddison, *The Gardener's Encyclopaedia of New Zealand Native Plants*, Godwit, Auckland, 1999

Chinery, Michael, *The Natural History of the Garden*, Collins, Glasgow, 1977

Clausen, Ruth Rogers and Nicholas H. Ekstrom, *Perennials for American Gardens*, Random House, New York, 1989

Clebsch, Betsy, *A Book of Salvias*, Timber Press, Portland, Oregon, 1997

Darke, Rick, *The Color Encyclopedia of Ornamental Grasses*, Timber Press, Portland, Oregon, 1999

Hobhouse, Penelope, *The Story of Gardening*. Dorling Kindersley, London, 2002

Huxley, Anthony (ed.), *The New Royal Horticultural Society Dictionary of Gardening*, Macmillan, London and Basingstoke, 1992

Lacey, Stephen, *The Startling Jungle*, Penguin, London, 1987

Lloyd, Christopher, *Clematis*, Collins, London, 1977
   The Well-Tempered Garden, Weidenfeld & Nicolson, London, 2003

Nichols, Clive, *Photographing Plants and Gardens*. David & Charles, Newton Abbot, Devon, 1994

Nelson, E. Charles, *An Irish Flower Garden*, Boethius Press, Kilkenny, 1984

Proctor, Rob, *Perennials – Enduring Classics for the Contemporary Garden*, Harper Collins New York, 1990

RHS Plant Finder 2007-2008, Dorling Kindersley, London, 2007

Thomas, Graham Stuart, *Perennial Garden Plants or The Modern Florilegium*, J. M. Dent, London, 1990; Frances Lincoln, London, 2004

Index

Entries in *italics* refer to illustration captions

OVERLEAF *Clematis* 'Romantika'

Acknowledgments

Author's Acknowledgments

With special thanks to Jo Christian, Anne Askwith and Becky Clarke of Frances Lincoln, Tom Fischer of Timber Press, and Diane Tomlinson, Mary Davies, Carmel Duignan, Mary Rowe, May Carmody, Tim Sharkey, Charles Nelson, Feargus McGarvey, Rob Proctor, Gerry Doran, Julie Dillon, Bill O'Sullivan, Dermot O'Neil, Assumpta Bloomfield, Rose Mary O'Brien, Rae McIntyre, Tom Duncan and Peter O'Connor.

Photographic Acknowledgments

©Paul Cusack: 8

©Helen Dillon: 1, 2–3, 4, 11, 12, 14, 16, 19, 21, 24, 25, 27, 31, 36, 47, 49, 50, 55, 61, 63, 64, 69, 72 right, 76 above, 76 below, 78, 80, 82 right, 84, 89, 94–5, 96, 99, 105, 107, 112, 114, 116, 121, 126, 132, 134, 144, 146, 150, 154, 157, 159, 160, 162, 165, 168, 172, 175, 176, 177, 178, 186, 191, 193, 195, 201, 203, 204 left, 204 centre, 204 right, 206–7, 209, 211, 212–13, 214, 215, 224

©Justine Pickett/papiliophotos.com: 123

©Rob Procter: 41, 43, 74, 82 left, 86, 139, 192, 196

©Diane Tomlinson: 6, 22, 35, 45, 53 left, 53 right, 58, 67, 70, 72 left, 101, 104, 108 above, 108 below, 110, 118 above, 118 below, 128, 131, 136, 152, 156, 167, 169, 173, 184, 188, 190